Walking with Muir across Yosemite

Thomas R. Vale
and
Geraldine R. Vale

The University of Wisconsin Press

The University of Wisconsin Press
1930 Monroe Street, 3rd floor
Madison, Wisconsin 53711-2059

3 Henrietta Street
London WC2E 8LU, England

www.wisc.edu\wisconsinpress

Printed in the United States of America

Library of Congress Cataloging-in-Publication Data
Vale, Thomas R., 1943–
Walking with Muir across Yosemite / Thomas R. Vale and Geraldine R. Vale.
176 pp.   cm.
Includes bibliographical references and index.
ISBN 0-299-15690-7 (cloth: alk. paper).
ISBN 0-299-15694-X (pbk.: alk. paper)
1. Natural history—California—Yosemite Valley.
2. Muir, John, 1838–1914.
I. Vale, Geraldine R.   II. Title.
QH105.C2V35   1998
508.794'47—dc21   97-20321

ISBN-13: 978-0-299-15694-7 (pbk.: alk. paper)

For our children,
Scott and Jackie,
and theirs—Hunter, Vanessa, Phyllicia, and McKenzie

"This is the way we like to travel—slowly, with lots of unplanned stops. So often the places along the way are nicer than where you're going."
—Scott Miles, in McCall, Idaho, 1996

Contents

Illustrations

Illustrations

Walking with Muir across Yosemite

1

Introduction

Among American conservationists, no name is more well-known, more revered, than that of John Muir. After publication of only two biographies earlier in this century, interest in Muir has blossomed over the last decade. Muir's words scroll across the placards of nature centers, Muir's politics weave through television specials, and Muir's meditations embellish the lavish photos of coffee-table picture books. Children's coloring books celebrate his life, and special editions of scientific journals analyze his activities and thoughts. Muir's books are republished with new covers and new introductions, his writings winnowed and sifted into vignettes on the water ouzel, the giant sequoias, or the southern Sierra. Like the later Aldo Leopold, John Muir is venerated by environmentally aware Americans eager to find wisdom among heroes of the past.

That adoration prompts a wealth of characterizations, some contradictory. Uncomplicated interpretations make him "father of our national park system," "climbing purist," or "typical Californian 'agribusinessman' of the late nineteenth century." Equally simplistically, his feats are touted, like those of a daredevil in a carnival sideshow, as "astounding, amazing, and almost unbelievable." More complex and sometimes enigmatic portrayals mold Muir into an early representative of contemporary political and ideological movements: "a radical amateur" who "spurned the scientific method," a person imbued with "radical egalitarianism," or a "deep ecologist" who "bears all the marks of constructive postmodernism." Still more philosophical characterizations hide Muir behind an abstruse veil: his living is said to represent "the Mahayana version of Buddhism, the Bodhisattva," or his worldview is described

3

John Muir standing beside and displaying the cone of a sugar pine. John Muir papers, Holt-Atherton Department of Special Collections, University of the Pacific Libraries. Copyright © 1984 Muir-Hanna Trust.

as derived from the "Divine Logos . . . [his ideas springing] full-grown from the Unconscious."

Gretel Ehrlich's introduction to the 1987 edition of Muir's *My First Summer in the Sierra*, although constructed with elegant prose, does little to lift the obscuring veil. Describing him as undergoing a profound change "with each vertical foot gained" in the mountains, Ehrlich suggests a reincarnation from "stern, solitary, and floundering" machinist and college drop-out, to a free spirit, "light as a banty rooster," whose prose suddenly "took on grace" as the "clean slate" of his previously "empty mind" apparently was "cleanly etched" by the beauty of the Sierra merely by the process of "absorb[ing] and absorb[ing]" as he "ramble[d] freely in the wilds." What Ehrlich finds "important" about Muir are his "acts of surrender"—through her eyes, he rises from those pages in *First Summer* a miraculous but passive Redeemer in the range.

With interpretations such as Ehrlich's, Muir becomes a remote and esoteric mystic, worthy of obscure scholarly study or cultlike reverence, but inaccessible to those less-philosophically inclined. For, alas, too few of us can hope to achieve Ehrlich's vision of Muir, for whom "Godliness was everywhere," as "up through the soles of his feet came the divinity of grasshoppers and granite, raindrops and water ousels."

What does one do, one wonders, to emulate Muir, to strive toward such transcendence through sole to soul? To answer this question, we have relived much of Muir's "first summer" in the Sierra, his own account of his experiences and impressions close at hand. We have found our companion to be treading a less fantastical, more earthly, path to understanding than many portray. We see Muir as acting not in submissive surrender to some mystic force but in dogged pursuit of empirical knowledge. We hear the "rhapsody" of Muir's "odes" floating not from the airy shepherd's pipe of a mythical Pan but from reeds tuned by more careful observation, more close study, more precise "dry reporting" than is commonly assumed. Indeed, his words and his actions hold promise for all of us who seek so "glorious conversion" that nature makes our "every nerve quiver, filling every pore and cell of us." All of us, like Muir, can be new Adams and Eves, intensifying our sojourn in nature's Paradise not by surrender and absorption but by investigation and understanding, always with respectful caring lest we be cast out for gaining knowledge without wisdom.

In this book, we hope to reemphasize the importance of natural history, of nature study, to John Muir's thinking and activity. We pursued our exploration of Muir by retracing the route that he followed during his "first summer in the Sierra." We did not attempt to replicate exactly in either space or time his precise footsteps; rather, we followed his route as modern visitors might, driving the roads and walking the trails that intersect with his route, reading Muir as we went along, looking for what Muir saw and contemplating, as best we could, how Muir might have reacted to the present landscape. Our objective was to discover Muir's approach to "recreation," to determine if that approach is still possible, and to wonder whether or not the modern visitor achieves Muir's engagement with the natural world.

In the pages that follow, we offer our analysis and reflections. Most generally our organization is chronological. First, a brief essay describes the basic natural history along the *First Summer* route in both Muir's time and our own. Then the heart of the book replicates the spatial flow of that route. Our chapters are entitled by, and focused upon, individual aspects of Muir's thought and behavior—observation, discovery, solitude, wildness, universality, rational romanticism, and brotherhood. These aspects might be described as the components of his experience,

Table 1.1. Relation of chapters in Muir's *My First Summer in the Sierra* to those in this book

Chapters in *First Summer*	Chapters in This Book
I. Through the Foothills with a Flock of Sheep	Observation
II. In Camp on the North Fork of the Merced	Observation
III. A Bread Famine	Observation
IV. To the High Mountains	Discovery
V. The Yosemite	Wildness
	Solitude
VI. Mount Hoffmann and Lake Tenaya	All Things, All Scales
VII. A Strange Experience	Rational Romanticism
VIII. The Mono Trail	Brotherhood
IX. Bloody Canyon and Mono Lake	Brotherhood
X. The Tuolumne Camp	Brotherhood
XI. Back to the Lowlands	Brotherhood

of his "recreation." In following Muir's summer route, we duplicate both his travel in the landscape and his presentation in the *First Summer* book (we focused our analysis on the 1987 Penguin edition), although not always chapter by chapter. Table 1.1 identifies the links between Muir's route and book and our own. Each of the chapters in this book repeats a certain structure: we first describe briefly Muir's location; then we analyze his writing to identify and explore a component of his experience; and finally we offer experiences of our own, sometimes a single narrative, sometimes several different, individual stories, in which we relate our encounters with nature that illustrate Muir's component. Each component builds upon the previous in the development of a holistic understanding of Muir, which is discussed, with policy implications for Yosemite, in a concluding essay.

Our personal involvements with Yosemite are long and rich, extending back more than two decades for one of us and half a century for the other. Our summers invariably include time in the high country, and a few years were dedicated to researching, writing, and publishing a book on stability and change in the Tuolumne landscape. For us, Yosemite will always be the most special and endearing of places.

That it was also so for Muir hardly needs mention. His attachment to this place was so profound, in fact, that it anchored him emotionally as well as physically, and it eventually led him away from the life of an inward-searching naturalist to that of an outward-looking activist. John Muir, born in Scotland in 1838, was the eldest son of Anne and Daniel

Thomas Vale in the Yosemite Sierra

Muir, who migrated to the United States to homestead farmland on the prairie of south-central Wisconsin in 1849. Young John suffered from a demanding, most today would say abusive, father whose religious fervor permitted little frivolity or even idleness and required almost constant, back-breaking toil. John's love of the natural world, clearly part of his Scottish childhood, flowered in the New World, where he also discovered talents at woodworking and inventive engineering. Opportunities to develop his interests were limited by the demands of father and farm, forcing Muir to carve out hours from sleep and inspiring him to devise a bed that tilted at the appointed hour to spill him to his feet and thus awaken him!

Leaving home in 1860 (to display his inventions at the state fair), John subsequently attended the state university in Madison (where he was befriended by Professors James Butler and Ezra Carr, and by Ezra's wife, Jeanne Carr, who would become his long-time mentor and confidante); wandered and worked in southern Canada (avoiding the Civil War draft); and then labored in an Indianapolis factory (where he was temporarily blinded by an errant metal file). His dream to follow the life-style and even the footsteps of Alexander von Humboldt, to travel the world in pursuit of nature study, prompted his abrupt resignation

Geraldine Vale in the Yosemite Sierra

in 1867 from the Indianapolis factory and the promising financial and commercial future it held.

Muir was off for the Amazon. His famous "thousand mile walk to the Gulf" was the first step in an intended life of wandering. A bout with malaria in Florida (a near-fatal experience) rendered him too weak to continue to South America, so, as a side-trip, a temporary deflection from his desired course, John traveled via steamship, and overland through Panama, to California, arriving in the spring of 1868. He spent eight days in Yosemite, but then overwintered as a tender of sheep at a ranch where the Sierra Nevada foothills meet the Great Central Valley. The subsequent summer in 1869, his "first summer in the Sierra," John was employed by a sheep rancher, Patrick Delaney, to oversee a sheepherder, "Billy," who was to guide a flock of sheep into progressively higher elevations of the Yosemite Sierra as the summer season advanced. This experience so engulfed John Muir's mind and soul that he rooted himself in Yosemite and northern California for the rest of his years.

Subsequent to the "first summer," he would walk and study in the Sierra for several additional years; begin publishing accounts of his scientific discoveries; marry in 1880; develop his wife's family fruit ranch at Martinez, located in the hills where the Sacramento and San Joaquin rivers empty into San Francisco Bay, into a commercial success; lead efforts on behalf of wild landscape protection; and travel widely, including a late-in-life venture into South America. But after 1869, California would remain home, and Yosemite would always be central to John Muir's sense of self. So also may it be for those of us who follow his example of observing, studying, reflecting, and caring, whether in the verdant valley meadows, across the rolling forested uplands, atop the gentle granite domes, or over the beckoning, serrated peaks of the land we call Yosemite.

2

The Natural Landscape

"How interesting everything is!" proclaimed Muir, thinking about the Yosemite Sierra. "Every rock, mountain, stream, plant, lake, lawn, forest, garden, bird, beast, insect seems to call and invite us to come and learn something of its history and relationship." And the same nature "calls" today, so effective has been the preservation of Yosemite since Muir's time. Changes have occurred, some reflecting the variability in the natural world, others prompted by human activities, but the nature that engaged Muir in 1869 would still be familiar to him today.

Even the Yosemite landscape of a century and a quarter ago was not purely natural. Burning, hunting, plant gathering, and village living by Native Americans altered the scene, particularly in certain locations —the old settlement sites at the mouth of Indian Canyon and near the present village development in Yosemite Valley being conspicuous examples. Still, the contemporary assertion—sufficiently popular to become unquestioned conventional wisdom—that the landscape was everywhere humanized, and therefore not "natural," overstates the effects of early peoples on the Yosemite landscape. In addition to Native Americans, moreover, initial European occupants had changed elements of the natural world prior to Muir's arrival: introduced grasses had much earlier replaced virtually all of the native grass species in the foothill environments; livestock grazed widely, including on the floor of Yosemite Valley; loggers harvested pines and firs in the forests (mostly at elevations lower than the present national park, but also in the valley itself); hydraulic mining for gold transformed miles of the riparian environments in the foothills into rolling seas of bare boulders; and grizzly bears and wolves had already been largely eliminated. Muir recorded many of these changes, but saw in the higher elevations of his

Yosemite Valley from the Big Oak Flat Road as it descends into the valley

First Summer journey a wild and natural landscape, and his vision was essentially accurate.

The relative persistence of the various elements of Yosemite's natural landscape since Muir's sojourn varies with the different paces of their natural dynamics and the degrees to which they are mutable by human activities. The most enduring and unchanging landscape element is the geological, whose forms are molded by processes that operate at time scales far longer than those of individual human lifetimes. Over the last twenty-five million years the massive block that is the Sierra Nevada has been uplifted—perhaps at an accelerating rate—along faults on the range's eastern front, the western side behaving more as a passive hinge; the uplift continues today, perhaps an inch or so per century. The resulting topography asymmetrically rises abruptly from the east, immediately cresting in Yosemite with peaks rising 11,000 to 13,000 feet above sea level (Mount Lyell is the highest point in the park at 13,114 feet), and then descends a long, gentle slope to the west. Streams flowing down the regional topographic slopes have dissected the uplifted block, carving a series of parallel, east-west–oriented canyons, short and steep on the eastern slope, long and gentle on the western. These west-side canyons deepen from the crest downstream, reaching their greatest depths in the middle elevations. In this sense at least, Yosemite Valley, at an elevation of 4,000 feet, is typical. The stream incision and the

11

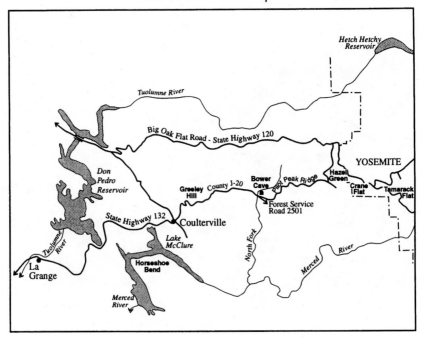

The contemporary landscape of Muir's *First Summer in the Sierra*. Map of Yosemite National Park by the University of Wisconsin—Madison Cartography Laboratory.

associated erosion on the valley sides caused by the downcutting has stripped off the old metamorphic rock (except in the foothills and in a linear band along, and east of, the crest) and exposed the younger igneous rock—the gleaming Sierran granites—that characterize most of the Yosemite landscape. Lacking a high density of cracks or fractures, the massive granites both maintain spectacularly steep slopes on the canyon walls and produce unusually rounded ridge tops and isolated rock monoliths—Half Dome and North Dome being common examples— by a mechanical weathering process called exfoliation.

During the last three million years (the cold period called the Pleistocene), ice fields on the Sierran crest gave birth to glaciers that flowed down the valleys, modifying the already rugged, stream-dissected landscape. Scraping away broken rock but unable to erode massive outcrops, which they polished to a fine shine, the glaciers exposed hard subsurface bedrock, deepened valleys, steepened slopes, and, more generally, accentuated the bold character of the landscape. The tongues of ice gouged out basins or constructed dams by deposition of eroded rock,

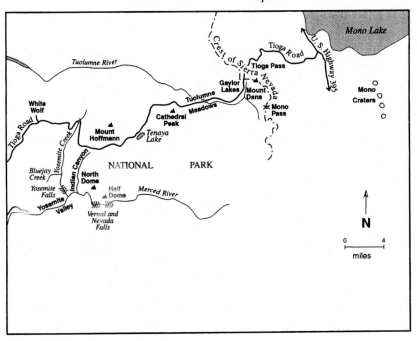

which allowed for the subsequent development of lakes. By differential erosion, either excavating rock broken by fractures or riding over rock massively hard and resistant, glaciers created irregular valley forms in the upstream-downstream direction, down which the post–Ice Age streams today alternately pool in quiet stretches and tumble through cascades and waterfalls.

Deep canyons, vast exposures of hard granite, polished rock surfaces, rounded domes, quiet lakes, cascading waterfalls—all of these features have changed little, if at all, since Muir first experienced them. So, too, with the basic patterns of generalized, day-to-day weather and year-to-year climate. The Sierra, like all of California, lies at a middle latitude and along the west coast of a continent, where alternating motion systems in the atmosphere bring contrasting seasons—warm and dry in the summer, mild and wet in the winter. (Muir, in the opening lines of his *First Summer* book, describes this two-season climate.) In the Sierra, summertime temperatures cool upward in elevation, from desiccating daytime heat in the foothills to moderate readings in the higher mountains. The loftier elevations also experience a break

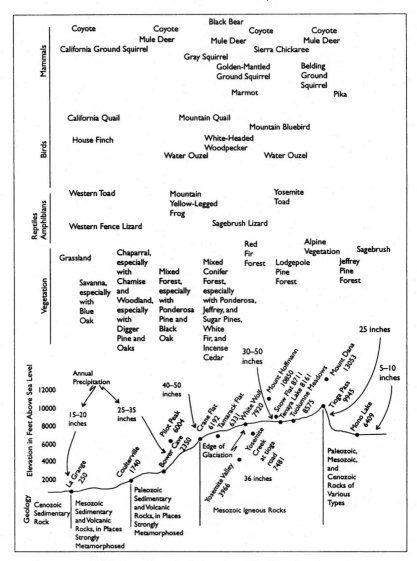

Some natural history characteristics along the *First Summer* route

in the unrelenting warm season drought of most of California when occasional surges of subtropical moisture from the Pacific Ocean or the Gulf of Mexico generate afternoon and evening thundershowers, sometimes with hail and downpours strong enough to close the park roads. Everywhere, however, precipitation that falls in the cool winter accounts for most of the annual totals. These values increase with elevation, at least to about 7,000 or 8,000 feet—from about 12 inches in the heart of the Central Valley, to 15 or 20 in the lower foothills, to 35 or 40 in the main forest belt (Yosemite Valley receives about 36 inches), and 40 to 50 in the higher elevations. The subalpine and alpine environments on the western slope may experience less precipitation than the upper middle elevations, but records are scarce. More clearly, the annual totals decline on the east side of the range: Ellery Lake, at the high elevation of 9,000 feet but east of Tioga Pass, receives only 25 inches. All locations, even the lower foothills, can be drenched in midwinter. For several of the cooler months, much of California, and particularly the west slope of the Sierra Nevada, receives more precipitation than most of the rest of the United States (the winter floods of 1996–1997 give testimony to the potentials of California's winter storms). Snowfall is heavy in the higher elevations— they are among the snowiest areas in the country—with maximum accumulated snow on the ground achieved by late March or early April. Tuolumne Meadows averages about 6 or 7 feet at that time, but other locations may accumulate much more: Snow Flat, for example, below Mount Hoffmann, recorded nearly 20 feet on the ground in late March 1983.

The melting snowpacks fill the streams and rivers for several months in late spring and early summer. The highest elevations warm later in the year, and that delayed thaw supports summer streamflows in these environments. The meager summer showers contribute relatively little runoff. Low flows or, at lower elevations, desiccated streambeds characterize late summer and fall.

The seasonal marches in weather and streamflow that the modern-day visitor experiences in the Yosemite Sierra are similar but not precisely identical to those that Muir knew. The middle to late 1800s were cooler and wetter than today, with larger summer snowfields and glaciers. Old photographs taken at the turn of the century reveal, for example, a much larger expanse of snow and ice in Mount Dana's Glacier Canyon than is seen now. By contrast, the particular year of Muir's *First Summer*, 1869, followed a winter of average precipitation, judging by the totals recorded in lowland California, including La Grange, where the *First Summer* journey began. Far more dramatic changes have occurred in the streamflow characteristics of the foothill rivers: The large dams on the Merced and Tuolumne rivers, by storing spring runoff and releasing it through the summer months, have made the downstream discharges less variable than in Muir's time.

The vegetation cover of the Sierra, as elsewhere, strongly reflects climate and soil water characteristics. The increase in annual precip-

Forest of red fir

itation with elevation supports a correspondingly taller, denser vegetation progressively upward through the middle elevations. These vegetation zones might be seen as drapes of north-south bands on the Sierran slopes, the edges of each band made irregular by the topographically influenced conditions of local climate and soil water. In the lowest foothills, several hundred feet above sea level, grasslands and, at slightly higher elevations, savannas and woodlands of blue oak cover the rolling landscape. On the first steep and rocky slopes, chaparral of chamise and manzanita replaces the grasses and savanna trees, and this dense shrub cover sweeps upward to higher terrain. On more gentle topography, at 2,000 to 3,000 feet in elevation, grows the mixed forest of oaks, particularly the deciduous black oak and the evergreen canyon and interior live oaks, and pines, notably the ponderosa and sugar pines; the "bench," as Muir described it, near Greeley and Bower Cave, exemplifies this forest. At still higher elevations, such as Yosemite Valley, this oak-pine forest is enriched with white fir and Douglas fir. On the slopes and valleys of the middle elevations, from about 6,000 to 7,000 feet—Crane Flat, for example—grows a forest of magnificent white fir, sugar pine, and Jeffrey pine, individual trees reaching skyward more than 200 feet. Above 8,000 feet, such as at Porcupine Flat, the dense forests of red fir, the largest of the world's true firs, dominate the spectacular forest belt. In the subalpine terrain (from Lake Tenaya through Tuolumne Meadows to Tioga Pass), the smaller lodgepole pine creates a dense, monotypic forest, which yields, on the highest peaks, ridges, and lake basins, to an alpine vegetation of low-growing, perennial herbaceous and woody plants and clumps of prostrate whitebark pine (krummholz). Along watercourses, especially in the lower and drier elevations, snake ribbons of riparian forest, and on the dry, rocky ridges and domes in the middle elevations, scattered trees (often Jeffrey pine and Sierra juniper) and shrubs root in cracks or depressions where weathered rock particles accumulate. A spring flush of herbaceous flowering plants spreads through the grasses and beneath the trees, the time of blooming advancing later in the year as the elevation increases.

This general pattern of vegetation—known to modern visitor and Muir alike—has been modified locally and in detail since 1869. Grazing, logging, road construction, home and recreational developments—all have altered the local pattern and character of foothill and lower mountain vegetation covers, although the broad bands in the plant cover remain. Within Yosemite National Park, fire suppression throughout most of this century has resulted in denser forest stands in the middle elevations (which formerly burned every decade or two) and in shifts in species compositions toward those trees favored by shade—incense cedar, white fir, and Douglas fir. In turn, the thicker forests, when they ignite, carry hot, stand-destroying fires; examples include the 1987 fire in the Bower's Cave region of the Merced River drainage and the 1990 fire between Crane Flat and the valley (the burned forest of which is conspicuous along the Big Oak Flat Road above the long tunnel). Fires played and continue to play little role in the higher elevation forests and meadows—from the red fir zone into the alpine landscape—but here the meadows have been heavily invaded by trees over the last century, likely a consequence of climatic warming and drying, perhaps encouraged by early sheep grazing. Unambiguously linked to climate, the timberline stands of lodgepole pine have increased in density, although the upper limit of forest growth seems stable, probably reflecting soil and topographic controls on that limit. Still, in spite of such changes and almost remarkably, given the growth in human numbers in the Yosemite landscape, the possibilities persist to experience the vegetation environments of 1869.

Some return to earlier vegetation conditions, even after more than a century of alteration, offers renewed opportunity to know nature. Fires again regularly burn in Yosemite, a result of either allowing lightning ignitions to burn or setting the vegetation aflame; any summer visitor to Yosemite Valley, for example, readily views the blackened bark, singed snags, and charred logs amid the new growth of tree seedlings, bracken, and wildflowers that characterize the forests made open and sunny by burning. Where fires cannot be used safely, such as adjacent to Yosemite Village, groves of black oak are being regenerated by planted seedlings. In the valley meadows, the afternoon wind again waves through chest-high grasses and flowering plants where Muir saw grazing cattle and men harvesting hay. Restoration has also returned the area of the old village, immediately downstream from the Sentinel Bridge, into a lush meadow. Along the Merced River, barrier fencing and willow planting attempt to reclaim streambanks denuded by human trampling, while logs, once removed from the water, now lie where they fall. In the higher elevations, trails are relocated from meadows, overused campsites closed and planted, and roadside disturbances revegetated with individual plants and clumps of meadow sod.

As is true for the vegetation, the fundamental pattern of wildlife populations similarly retains its mid–nineteenth-century character—a pattern strongly reflective of the Sierra's persisting elevational ordering of vegetation and climate—although animal species may have changed more since Muir's *First Summer* year than any other part of the landscape. Among the mammals, mule deer might be more numerous than in the past, benefiting from the improved browse resulting from logging outside the park. Black bears, too, may have expanded their range as a consequence of the demise of the grizzly bear and the introduction of food by people; coyotes may have similarly benefited from the loss of the wolf. Some species have likely declined—bighorn sheep because of the usurping of their grazing range and the introduction of diseases, (the 1986 reintroduction of bighorns to the LeeVining Creek drainage was set back by high mortality during the severe winters of the mid-1990s), and wolverine (never common) perhaps because of sensitivity to humans in their alpine haunts. The mix of bird species persists as in Muir's day, but in certain locations declines in numbers are conspicuous. In Yosemite Valley, many vireos, warblers, and flycatchers suffer from the nest parasitism of brown-headed cowbirds; in the higher forests, great gray owls likely find fewer quiet, midelevation meadows in which to nest and hunt; peregrine falcons persist only in small numbers in their cliff environments. In recent years, amphibians in Yosemite have declined precipitously, as they have in many, perhaps most, parts of not only California but the world.

Human interactions with animals in Yosemite nonetheless remain rich and varied, as they were for Muir. Bears are less in evidence, a success story of Park Service efforts to convince visitors of the virtues of proper food storage. But the possibilities of encountering bears in the wild landscape remain: One of our finest such meetings involved a large black bear, water droplets dangling from its dark hair and glistening in the sun, as it ambled up from Yosemite Creek, surprising us and we it. We stared at each other across a distance of 10 feet before the bear turned and ran rapidly off. Chipmunks, marmots, and ground squirrels enliven visitor days in the valley, on Glacier Point, at Olmsted Point, and in the campgrounds. Steller's jays and black-headed grosbeaks crowd the picnic tables in the middle elevations, Clark's nutcrackers at Olmsted Point. Away from the crowded campgrounds and busy highway pull-outs, habitats are still as rich in birds as in Muir's day—streams for as many reclusive solitary dippers; forests for as many raucous woodpeckers (like the black-backed three-toed that we added to our life list with a sighting along the Cathedral Lake trail); high-elevation snowbanks for as many fluttering rosy finches; and quiet perches, meadow borders, or open skies for species of hawks (including the northern goshawk that we watched several evenings along the edge of Tuolumne Meadows near Soda Springs).

Taken together, then, the elements of nature in the Yosemite landscape, however modified in detail, retain the fundamental characteristics that Muir knew. The modern visitor can still find the natural world vital and vigorous, rich and boundless. Its "call" continues, "invit[ing] us to come and learn."

3

Observation

*To learn something of the plants,
animals, and rocks*

On June 3, 1869, John Muir left French Bar, on the Tuolumne River, at the very edge of the foothills of the Sierra Nevada. His companions were 2,050 sheep, at least 3 dogs, and 4 other men: the owner, Mr. Delaney, "the Don"; Billy, "the proud shepherd"; and "a Chinaman and a Digger Indian to assist in driving for the first few days." They sought higher elevations where the sheep could forage in greener fields. For the first five days the band of animals and men plodded through the heat and dust of the California summer where "every plant had been roasted in an oven." They wandered lost through the "thorny jungle" of chaparral, emerged onto the lowest rugged mountain slopes near Horseshoe Bend on the Merced River, passed uneventfully through the village of Coulterville, and then ascended to the lower edge of the coniferous forest near Greeley's Mill. Beyond Bower's Cave, they made camp in the narrow, deep valley of the North Fork of the Merced River. For a full month, the sheep fed on the "ceanothus brush on the hills and tufted grass patches here and there," tended only by the sheepherder and Muir. His responsibilities minimal, Muir used his time to explore the brushy slopes and forest groves on Pilot Peak Ridge, the "glad exulting onsweeping currents" of the river, and the boundless sky overhead.

🌲🌲🌲🌲🌲🌲🌲🌲🌲🌲🌲🌲🌲🌲🌲🌲🌲🌲🌲🌲🌲🌲🌲

Although Muir wrote that he would have accepted "work of any kind" that summer to allow him time in the Yosemite region, the job of shep-

21

herd overseer seemed to offer the specific appeal of leaving him "perfectly free to follow [his] studies." He reasoned that the long stops at progressive camps seeking fresh forage as it emerged from the warming soil would offer "good centers of observation" from which "to learn something of the plants, animals, and rocks." Two of the four camping "provisions" that he mentions are a plant press and a notebook, which he tied to his belt. Muir laments the shepherd, in contrast, who rarely had "much good mental work or recreation in the way of books" and returned to his "dingy hovel cabin at night, stupidly weary," with "nothing to balance and level his life with the universe." Muir himself, however, set out energetically to "study plants and rocks and scenery as much as [he] liked."

Throughout the text of this portion of his book, as indeed elsewhere in *My First Summer*, Muir generally comments initially on the daily vicissitudes of the weather and, though less often, describes or interprets the more stable geology. He typically provides a brief objective overview, continues with particular details, and concludes with a personalized interpretation, sometimes an apt metaphor, more often long passages in the highly imaginative, Romantic style of which he was so fond. Usually quoted by his interpreters are the latter lines of figurative language; often eschewed are the more lengthy empirical observations that inspired them.

The first paragraph of the book establishes a point of contrast for the ensuing days. Muir had recently completed a winter's work in the French Bar area at the edge of the Central Valley, where "there are only two seasons—spring and summer." He notes the months of rain, the months of seasonal drought, ending with a metaphor for a valley summer that relates the natural landscape to a situation familiar to everyone, when it appeared that "every plant had been roasted in an oven."

Admittedly, figurative language abounds in Muir's descriptions of the weather generally. To him, clouds are less often cumulus or stratus than "floating fountains," "sky mountains," or "landscapes of the sky," but Muir had little background to report atmospheric conditions in scientific terms and the total lines devoted to the atmosphere, although quite quotable, are typically brief compared to other topics. Moreover, he often perceives the elements of atmosphere in metaphors of the flora or fauna, more familiar to him, and with regard to weather's effect on the land below: lightning sparks like "quick-throbbing fireflies in the Wisconsin meadows" and stars bloom like "sky lilies." A reversal of his usual detail/reflection style, an observation of the rain's effect on plants,

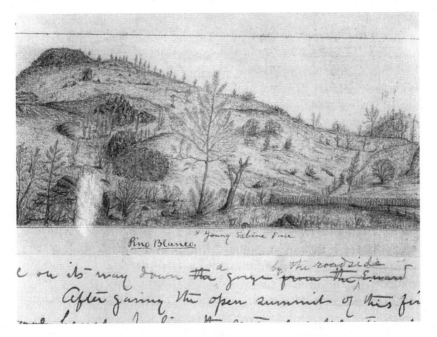

Muir sketch of Pino Blanco. John Muir papers, Holt-Atherton Department of Special Collections, University of the Pacific Libraries. Copyright © 1984 Muir-Hanna Trust.

streams, lakes, and rocks, follows his exuberant lauding of the cloudy "world building" of the sky. A paragraph opening with exclamations about the "celestial" nature of air currents shifts halfway through to notes of their failure to sway "a single lily on its stalk" in the camp below at the North Fork of the Merced, and ends with what might be an entry in a botanical textbook: "The species is *Lilium pardalinum*, five to six feet high, leaf-whorls a foot wide, flowers about six inches wide, bright orange, purple spotted in the throat, segments revolute—a majestic plant." A day later, his opening tribute to the "mountains of the sky" concludes with a direct floral analogy: "One may fancy the clouds themselves are plants, springing up in the sky fields at the call of the sun, growing in beauty until they reach their prime, scattering rain and hail like berries and seeds, then withering and dying." Two full weeks go by with only a couple of dozen lines relating generally to the weather before Muir starts to hone his observations to the more specific percentage of cloud cover: ".05 of the sky [in clouds at noon June 18] about .75 in all. . . . Periodical shower-bearing cumuli . . . [and] thin diffused, fog-like cloud overhead [on June 22]. . . . Average cloudiness

23

for day about .25 [on June 30]." Scant other references to the sky occur within these remaining twenty days at the North Fork camp except a final, brief tribute to the "alabaster cloud-mountains" in his last entry.

Muir's references to geology are more specific and literal, although even less frequent than those to the sky. As the sheepherding party leaves French Bar, he describes the "foothills of metamorphic gold-bearing slates dip[ping] below the stratified deposits of the Central Valley." This observation stands alone without further comment as do the ensuing ones of the "outcropping masses of slate" emerging in the foothill grasslands "in sharp lichen-covered slabs like tombstones in deserted burying grounds" and later the "carefully sandpapered" ridges in the view from Horseshoe Bend. The latter quotation concludes a rather lengthy view of the rising landscape generally, and although he continues with an emotional "How wonderful the power of its beauty! Gazing awestricken, I might have left everything for it," Muir confirms that the ultimate nature of his relationship with this wilderness would be one of "glad but endless work . . . tracing the forces that have brought forth its features, its rocks and plants and animals and glorious weather"—a sentiment surely more befitting a natural scientist than a mystic seer.

His text is rich with accounts of Sierra's fauna. Although much chagrined by the domestic "hoofed locusts" that "devoured . . . almost every leaf . . . within a radius of a mile or two from camp," Muir delighted in his experiences with other living creatures: lizards (forty-seven lines), "[liking] them the better the longer one looks into their beautiful innocent eyes"; the "small savage black ant" (thirty-eight lines); the more "laborious" and more docile "large jet-black ants" (forty-eight lines); the "fine, active intelligent-looking red ants" (six lines); the "beautiful" large California gray squirrel (forty-five lines); the smaller Douglas squirrel (twenty-one lines); and the squirrel-like wood rat (sixty-four lines). Like another famous lover of nature who focused attention on ants, Henry David Thoreau, Muir gives close attention to the behavior of the tiny species that he observes. Absent, however, are the many historical and mythical allusions of "Battle of the Ants," which the earlier writer used in his lengthy comparison to civilization's bloody predilections. Muir's journal entries are more about "natural" history, and, although they include real "acquaintances" with the reptiles, insects, and mammals sure to be encountered by most travelers, focus on more detached identification and nesting, feeding, and "work" habits. Birds receive less attention, except for a major entry about a diving "dipper," a species whose appearance and behavior Muir reported carefully (thirty-two lines).

Muir's talents as a naturalist are perhaps most evidenced by his concentration of endless work on Yosemite's flora, particularly the trees. "Would I could understand them!" he exclaims, and though he is "never weary of gazing" at their grandeur, believing "every tree calls for special admiration," his way of appreciating them is by "measuring" their height, their circumference, their cones; by "making many sketches and regret[ting] that [he] cannot draw every needle"; by becoming so rapt in his sketches at times as to be startled by an Indian arriving from nearby Brown's Flat approaching to "within a few steps" of him in camp. From the foothills to the edge of the forest, Muir describes each new tree species encountered, identifying it with both common and scientific names: first the blue oak (*Quercus douglasii*), as already mentioned on the first day, then the "palm-like," gray digger pine (*Pinus sabiniana*) on the second near Coulterville, with nineteen lines of natural history, which he is so "eager to sketch" that he is in a virtual "fever of excitement." On June 6, he records the displacement of blue oak with black (*Quercus kelloggii*), "at a height of about 2,500 feet . . . at the edge of the great coniferous forest," taking care to distinguish its "deeply lobed deciduous leaves, picturesquely divided trunk, and broad, massy, finely lobed and modeled head." Juxtaposed with these relatively "dry" data, in fact, are the much-quoted lines, "We are now in the mountains and they are in us. . . . Our flesh-and-bone tabernacle seems transparent as glass to the beauty about us as if truly an inseparable part of it. . . . How glorious a conversion!" It is noteworthy that such close study spawns so swiftly Muir's exuberance, and also that he is inspired to such "graceful" prose when the snow-covered peaks of Yosemite are first visible in the distance. Such language, written before his first footfall above the foothills, belies Gretel Ehrlich's assertion that Muir's "rhapsodic" prose was engendered by the climb into the heights beyond. In fact, Muir's imagery is fairly comparable to that of the literary master he so admired, Ralph Waldo Emerson, in his poetic "I Become a Transparent Eyeball" in *Nature*.

On the afternoon of the same day, thirty lines are devoted to the natural history of the "feathery," mammoth-coned sugar pine (*Pinus lambertiana*) and later in the same entry thirteen lines to the bare-trunked, flat-plumed, yellow-green, aromatic incense cedar (*Calocedrus decurrens*), each followed by rather straightforward asides of about five lines. Later, for the "mountain" live oak (*Quercus chrysolepis*), twenty-two lines

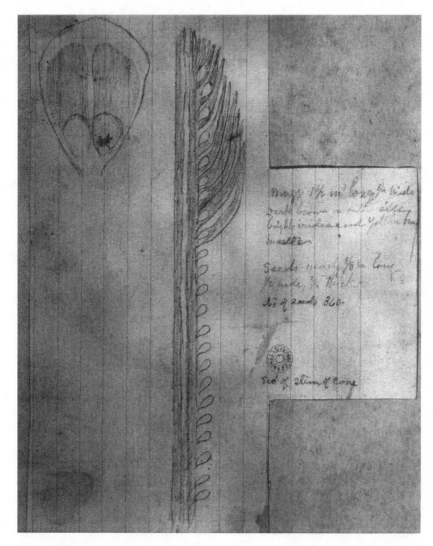

Muir sketch of a pine cone. John Muir papers, Holt-Atherton Department of Special Collections, University of the Pacific Libraries. Copyright © 1984 Muir-Hanna Trust.

carefully document statistics of size, branching form, leaf shape, and acorn cups, and for a passage about both sugar and yellow pine, an impressive fifty-seven lines; both are supplemented with fine sketches useful for identification in the field.

Despite Muir's fascination with trees, his appreciation of much less lofty flora is almost as strong. From a vantage point at Horseshoe Bend, he stands transfixed for hours before a stretch of chamise chaparral, "a heaving, swelling sea of green." Later, he "examines" this "dense, almost impenetrable growth" of the rose family shrub (accurately noting the plant's taxonomic relationship), reaching 6 to 8 feet in height and, in early June, bedecked with "small white flowers in racemes eight to twelve inches long," along with its associate manzanita (*Arctostaphylos*), Mariposa lilies, and species of Brodiaea, for a total of twenty-three lines, relying on the scientific "*Adenostoma fasciculata*" over the more informal "chamise." Moreover, Muir sketched his careful notes not while blithely swaying from a tree but typically while quietly seated on a stable boulder.

The following paragraph, in contrast, speaks rather briefly about the "charming," "showy," and "fragrant" "*Azalea occidentalis*," identifying it by comparison to the more familiar (to Muir, at least) rhododendron and by description of its habitat along cool streams amid alders, willows, and ferns: "We found it this evening in bloom a few miles above Greeley's Mill. It is . . . very showy and fragrant." Yet what a contrast to Emerson's poem "Rhodora," in which the figurative language so obscures the subject that many of today's high school students are at a loss to identify the subject as a flower! Apparently Muir saw his "Godful work" to be observing closely as a learner, and later in his guidebooks communicating clearly as a teacher, before he felt "worthy" to be a spokesperson for Yosemite. After describing in sixteen lines the profuse poison oak (*Rhus diversiloba*), he appears to wax anthropocentric in asking why such a plant, "not apparently useful to man" and "somewhat troublesome to most travelers," was made, but the query is merely rhetorical. Muir concludes that "first of all it might have been made for itself"—fine biocentric reasoning.

Twenty-five days at the North Fork of the Merced afforded Muir even more opportunity to botanize. Camped in a bowery haven in "a picturesque hollow formed by converging hill slopes at a bend of the river," Muir luxuriated in the "glorious array" of "spring works" called forth by "starry compositae, monardella, Mariposa tulips, gilias, violets." Later, clarkia, coreopsis, and lupine "unroll" and "unfold" along the river's banks and beyond the reaches of the "handsome little shrub, *Chamaebatia foliosa*" (mountain misery), which he describes in typical Muir fashion:

> Belonging to the rose family, [it] spreads a yellow-green mantle beneath the sugar pines for miles without a break. . . . This fine carpet shrub begins to appear at, say, twenty-five hundred or three thousand feet

above sea level, is about knee high or less, has brown branches, and the largest stems are only about half an inch in diameter. The leaves, light yellow green, thrice pinnate and finely cut, give them a rich ferny appearance, and they are dotted with minute glands that secrete wax with a peculiar pleasant odor that blends finely with the spicy fragrance of the pines. The flowers are white, five eighths of an inch in diameter, and look like those of the strawberry.

The "leafy tunnel" of the streamside especially drew Muir, where he could "fain draw every leaf . . . and every curved and spotted petal" of the large orange lily, *Lilium pardalinum*. Repeatedly he returns to written studies of these flowers and "their rhizomes . . . set in black mould accumulated in hollows of the metamorphic slates." From first mentioning the plants a scant week earlier, Muir begins to refer to them as "my" lily gardens.

Few major plant species seem to escape Muir's keen eye—the "showy involucres of flowering dogwood" (eighteen lines), the "purple . . . tall glandular racemes" of the giant saxifrage (thirteen lines), the "soft and hairy" leaves of the "beaked hazel." But the one that turns this "botanist wild with admiration" is the "commonest and most widely distributed of all the ferns," *Pteridium aquilinum*, more commonly, bracken. This "commonest fernstuff," notably little described except for its 7-foot measurement of "arching branching ribs and veins" is sufficient to create a "fairyland." Muir laments the common failure to share his joy of merely sitting quietly beneath its fronds: "I sat a long time beneath the tallest fronds, and never enjoyed anything in the way of a bower of wild leaves more strangely impressive. . . . It would seem impossible that any one, however incrusted with care, could escape the Godful influence of these sacred fern forests. Yet this very day I saw a shepherd pass through one of the finest of them without betraying more feeling than his sheep."

Muir seemed satisfied at this camp to identify, document, and revel in the quiet study of known plant species. His journal entries give no indication of any efforts to anchor his name to any of the "many ill-defined species" of lupine. Putting notebook to rest for the night, he turns himself to sleep beneath dogwood and alder, among foambells and lilies, on an 8-foot "altar" of an ancient granite boulder in the middle of the stream, "the most romantic spot [he] had yet found . . . where one might hope to see God."

Observation

For Muir, the starting point for his *First Summer* journey was a place "where the foothills of metamorphic gold-bearing slates dip below the stratified deposits of the Central Valley." Topographically, it is a point where the modern traveler leaves the flat, alluvial plain and begins to cross the lowest foothills. Probably in 1869 and certainly today, it is also the transition in land use from the irrigated row crops and orchards on the west to the wild landscapes of rangeland and forest on the east. Wildness dominates the entire length of the *First Summer* route.

Today's La Grange, in Muir's time called French Bar, perches on a stream terrace above the south side of the Tuolumne River. Several dozen homes, mostly older wooden frame structures, quietly sit beneath an open canopy of trees—small ailanthus and valley oaks; a couple of large, ragged date palms; and a line of recently planted, purple-leaved flowering plums—that stand out amid the surrounding dry grassland. Numerous "For Sale" signs plead release for the tenants from the unrelenting heat. The main street fronts the only operating businesses, a bar and grill and a small grocery. Sitting abandoned are a hotel, a gas station, and a restaurant whose new, rough-wood front made to look "Western" apparently had not drawn in the hungry hordes. Dogs bark from beyond the stores, back among the trees and modest homes; a couple stand chatting in front of the bar; a wanderer searches the trash can by the river for aluminum cans. Cars and pickups and vans and motor homes pass through, although few stop. The town is a little too far east to benefit from the irrigated fields of the Central Valley, too far west (and too isolated) to prosper from the recreation in the mountains, too lacking in resources to expand with the revival of gold mining (which ended here after the hydraulic boom of the 1870s), too remote (at least for the moment) to grow as a bedroom for the Bay Area. It has the ragged, unpolished look of a former foothill mining camp set in a Central Valley landscape.

Heading eastward toward the Sierra, State Highway 132 leaves La Grange in two sharp right-angle turns as the pavement rises from the alluvial bench onto the low swells of the foothills that roll toward the distant mountains. Quickly crossing a canal that sucks water from the Tuolumne River in order to sustain crops in the valley bottom farther south and west, the smooth asphalt speeds into the golden waves of desiccated grasses. The arid summer heat, baking the vegetation until "it is dead and dry and crisp" and "making everything dreary," is as "hard to bear" as in Muir's time. But whereas the sheep and sheep-tenders alike confronted "smothering dust," we are unstressed by the elements in the comfort of an air-conditioned car and confident that we will cross the oven in an hour, rather than over several days on foot, relieved that we need not make a "dry" camp here for the night. The only dust we raise blows in a low dense cloud as we pull off the highway onto the unpaved road shoulder.

The landscape presents a kaleidoscope of earth tones—dull brown to bronze to gold—interrupted by the splashes of bright green sedges and willows along watery seeps and occasional patches of reddish-brown poison oak emerging several feet above the yellow grass. The gray and black of the metamorphic rock crops out on the roadcuts. Blue oaks—"with pale blue-green leaves and white bark"—remain "sparsely planted" in an open oak savanna, still often rooted, as Muir noted, "in the crevices of rocks," but more generally without obvious pattern or relationship to the topography. Low mounds of gray leaves mark individual turkey mullein plants that line the edge of the pavement. As they did for Muir, the beds of upturned slates impress us. In places, gray shards with red and green lichen graffiti emerge from the soil

Blue oaks, grassland, and upturned metamorphic rocks, east of La Grange

like ancient, age-bent gravestones; in others, taller spires soar like the skyscrapers of a miniature city. Pulling back onto the pavement, giving birth to still another cloud of dust, with our air conditioner on high, we once again race eastward across the "oveny" scene.

The torrid landscape is hardly without the cheerfulness of life. Whereas Muir noted "cottontail rabbits . . . running from shade to shade" and "magpies and crows . . . with bill[s] wide open and wings drooped, too breathless to speak," we see western kingbirds clinging to the barbed wire of the roadside fence with skulking unconcern for the glaring heat, and a few horned larks scavenging turkey mullein seeds from the gravel road shoulder. A western meadowlark perches on a fence post. An acorn woodpecker edges up the side of a wooden power pole toward a red-tailed hawk on its crowning cross-arm; a mourning dove looks down from the connecting wire. From a blue oak peals a mockingbird's melodious voice, while high overhead another hawk harasses a turkey vulture. Instead of "long-eared hares . . . cantering gracefully," we find the silvery-gray California ground squirrels, motionless sentries gazing from fence posts, even those of slender steel.

The hot, dry rangeland, although not as wild as in Muir's day, is relatively free of human settlement. The fences and utility lines are our constant trail guides. Several dozen homes swelter in the heat as the road rises into the increasingly hilly and dense oak woodland. A roadside store beckons passing boaters and waterskiers, temporary denizens of the nearby reservoir waters, with promises of cold colas and refreshing beer. But whereas Muir endured the constant companionship of two thousand domestic sheep, panting "pitifully" in the heat, we see only a few horses standing with drooped tails in the sun and a herd of several dozen Hereford huddled beneath the shade of a particularly massive, sprawling blue oak. Sheep have long since disappeared from prominence in the California, and Western, range economy.

The highway rises over a low ridge, then falls to skirt the water of Don Pedro Reservoir before it sweeps upward on a west-facing slope on which we note, among the blue oaks, just where Muir also encountered them, the first dark green patches of chamise chaparral and gray-green digger pines. Chamise, the most abundant member of the foothill chaparral, still forms "a dense, almost impenetrable growth . . . six to eight feet high." In his coat buttonhole, Muir wore the plant's "pretty fragrant racemes . . . of small white flowers," but we who pass by later in the summer season admire instead from afar the reddish tinge that the drying flowers lend to the green blanket of shrubs. The tall digger pines, with trunks that divide "at a height of fifteen or twenty

31

feet into two or more stems, outleaning or nearly upright with many straggling branches and long grey needles," suggested to Muir more "a palm than a pine." We do not see the resemblance, but welcome this frequent associate of blue oak and chamise brush of lowland California.

At the ridge summit, on Pino Blanco, what Muir described as the "first bench" of the foothills, the east-bound traveler suddenly encounters the first vista that deserves the description "mountainous." Two thousand feet of gray rock and undulating waves of dark green chamise chaparral rise from the great Horseshoe Bend of the Merced River valley, its lowest levels now drowned beneath the reservoir surface of Lake Mc-Clure. In spite of the human alteration, the scene impresses us as much as it did Muir: "Bold, down-sweeping slopes, feathered with pines . . . fold beyond fold of finely modeled hills and ridges rising into mountain-like masses . . . , all covered with a shaggy growth of chaparral, mostly adenostoma [chamise] . . . a heaving swelling sea of green as regular and continuous as that produced by the heaths of Scotland."

Boaters and waterskiers drive the access road to the Horseshoe Bend Recreation Area toward the inviting coolness of the lake, but we pause along its shady length to reflect on Muir's admiration for this landscape's "lavish richness of detail . . . its rocks and plants and animals and glorious weather." An arbor of interior live oak, valley oak, digger pine, and willow arches over the tinkle of a tiny creek with its bordering thicket of shrubs—toyon, spicebush, and poison oak—rooted in the gravels and cobbles of the valley bottom site. Grape vines, lush with clusters of green fruit, send their translucent purple stems climbing over everything—trees, shrubs, and recreation area signs—engulfing all in leafy green. Tiger swallowtails flutter gently about. A California quail caw-caws from a bushy lookout; a rufous-sided towhee trills and a chat whistles from deep within the tangle, answered by the staccato of the wrentit. From the trees overhead, we hear the whistling of a plain titmouse and glimpse ash-throated flycatchers and linnets. A flash of yellow, black, and gray—Lawrence's goldfinches sing canary-like as they alternately soar and glide from tree to tree and from tree to browned grasses and thistles. The intense dry heat in an utterly featureless and cloudless sky is softened only by a slight breeze.

Leaving the lowland of reservoir and shady arbor, the highway climbs upward in a grade made gentle by modern construction standards, through stands of chamise chaparral, before emerging onto an upland of blue oak, golden grasses, and the gold-rush town of Coulterville. Only mentioned in passing by Muir, the settlement receives more attention from modern visitors. Desires for a hamburger or pizza, ice

Chaparral of chamise with digger pine, west of Coulterville

cream or cola, prompt brief stops, while the old Jeffrey Hotel encourages an overnight stay in a building whose 30-inch-thick walls of rock and adobe dating back to 1851 looked down on Muir and his sheep in 1869. The several blocks of the old main street, bordered by handsome buildings of a bygone era, stretch subdued and reserved in the midsummer heat, largely lacking the amenities that have transformed most sizable towns in the Sierra foothills into tourist meccas of the late twentieth century. The traffic is sufficiently sparse that only a little imagination conjures an image of two thousand sheep herded unobstructed up the sizzling pavement.

Beyond Coulterville, the highway again climbs, at first gently through oak woodlands, the first few ponderosa pine, and a line of white alders, sinking their roots into a moist streamside, and then more steeply, amid the densest chamise and manzanita chaparral yet. Muir found these stands of shrubs to be "unbroken" by trees (a characteristic that he attributed to frequent burning), whereas we are impressed by the scattered digger pine that protrude handsomely above the blanket of brush, their long, feathery needles glistening in the morning light. Still higher, on the ridgetop above, the first forest stands in outline against the blue sky. Within a few tenths of a mile from the summit, and 5.5 miles above Coulterville, we encounter, just where Muir did, "the edge of the great coniferous forest" where it laps over the crest. Here are the first dense stands of ponderosa pine and the first of its common associates, the sugar pine and incense cedar.

This grade carries the traveler from foothills to mountains. On a clear day, most likely in the spring when a good rain and a following wind have cleared the air, the view back to the west can be spectacular. We luckily encounter such a day in mid-summer, at the end of a week during which subtropical moisture had surged over central California. Heavy rains had fallen from Tioga Pass to Yosemite's western entrance at Hodgdon Meadow, and the thick deck of clouds had even extended down over the foothills as far as Oakdale, cooled one morning by a rare July mist. We look out now more than 100 miles through a cleansed sky, from the dark green chaparral at our feet, across the tawny grass clearing of Coulterville and the rolling slopes of brush and oak woodlands beyond, to the dried grassland fringing the Central Valley and the irrigated lands extending into the already-forming typical summer haze. On the horizon rise the Coast Ranges, probably in the vicinity of San Jose or San Francisco, dark and distant against the bright western sky. Although we examine the nearby blackish slates exposed in the road cuts and the chaparral shrubs blanketing the rock, our attention is drawn back to the view over which we, like Muir, "gazed and gazed and longed and admired."

At the top of the grade, on what Muir called "the second bench or plateau of the Range," the road flattens out. Over the next 8 or 9 miles, it still occasionally rises in short climbs through pine and brush but often runs over rolling surfaces or valley bottoms of forest and golden grassland. On the very first such grassy flat, immediately beyond the summit, we see what greeted Muir: "through a meadow opening in the pine woods . . . [the] snowy peaks about the headwaters of the Merced above Yosemite." Farther on, in another large, forest-rimmed valley, where the late-blooming, pink-purple farewell-to-spring part the dried grasses, we spot a coyote combing for rodents. A few minutes later, a couple of loud cracks—we assume gunshots—break the stillness, and we wonder if a local has also discovered the animal and found it more intrusive. Buildings are scattered about in the forest and beside the grassy openings, with a few small stores clustered at the road junction called Greeley Hill. The road becomes progressively more primitive.

Observation

The State Highway 132 was left behind at Coulterville, and County Highway J-20, which began where the state highway ended, now curves off to the north. The road narrows in its ascent, at first with a good but heavily patched asphalt surface, then with an oiled veneer. Abruptly, where Forest Service roads 2S01 and 2S05 meet, just beyond the bridge crossing of the North Fork of the Merced River, the pavement ends.

The increased primitiveness of the road echoes the increased wildness in the landscape beyond Greeley Hill. Distances between buildings increase; cultivated fields and planted trees stretch further apart. The topography is more rugged. Swept over by intense, widespread fire a few years before, the slopes of forest and brush rise in wild, uneven patterns. Traffic on the road is almost nonexistent. The modern traveler can appreciate Muir's assessment of the last century that here one feels "in the mountain's heart."

We linger, as we often do at this spot where the pavement yields to gravel, never failing to find a rich and vibrant nature. A wealth of mountain and foothill trees mingle: Ponderosa pine and incense cedar, a few sugar pine and Douglas fir, grow with blue oak, interior live oak, and digger pine. The shrubs are mostly those associated with the foothills, including poison oak, ceanothus, and manzanita. Among the trees and shrubs, especially in the open vegetation enhanced by a fire, a wealth of flowering plants bloom, both native and introduced—California poppy and mustard; farewell-to-spring and star thistle; buckwheat and mullein; phacelia, milkweed, and lupine, with pods of ripening seeds. Insects abound. White cabbage and yellow swallowtail butterflies pepper the air; little blue butterflies draw nectar from tawny buckwheat flowers; polychromatic dragonflies dart about in rapid flight. Birds are everywhere—feeding, singing, displaying, resting. Mourning doves perch in the branches of the last trees of an old orchard, an acorn woodpecker sits on the bole of a tall, dead digger pine, and goldfinches feast on the downy seeds of the thistle. Swallows pursue their insect prey on the wing, an Anna's hummingbird gyrates in its distinctive aerial display, and a wood peewee languidly screeches its raspy note repeatedly from the branch of a ponderosa pine. Western fence lizards scurry across the monument commemorating the Coulterville Road into Yosemite—a monument built of what we think might be serpentinite rock—and California ground squirrels dart noisily through the dried grasses from fence post to burrow. At the bridge, where we look down into the lazy flow of water shaded by alder and willow, we catch the shadows of fish darting about, a few occasionally jumping after insects, and hear the call note, we surmise, of a yellow-breasted chat. The dry air is always warm, often hot, on summer days, filled with the fragrance generated by desiccating heat.

The sky overhead is typically clear, not benefiting from the cloud buildups that grace the higher elevations, but it is invariably etched by jet trails of planes high overhead. At first narrow and distinctly linear, these pencil-thin clouds gradually become more broad and ragged as the winds disperse the condensation until they seem to be bands of cirrus clouds produced by entirely natural means. We think of them metaphorically as suggesting the power of nature to obliterate the human marks on the landscape around us: the abandoned orchard (though still managing to produce a few green pears) gradually dying out; the old concrete foundations of lodging built for travelers on the way to Yosemite crumbling under gravity's inexorable force; the Bower Cave, just upslope, which once welcomed visitors with a constructed dance floor and a pool large enough to warrant a boat, now resting alone, its gaping entrance of marble boulders abandoned by all but encroaching poison oak; the cracked road pavement with weedy plants anchoring themselves amid the oiled surface; the mounds of gophers reclaiming the asphalt shoulder. Even the strongest nearby reminders of the human capacity to dominate nature—the robust fence of steel posts and barbed wire and the concrete road bridge—are hardly new and modern. We wonder what Muir would think. Would he find at this spot a reassurance that "nature is doing what she can, replanting, gardening, . . . patiently trying to heal every raw scar"? Or would he be dismayed by the jet trails in a sky that he thought, once the earth's surface had been humanized, alone would be "safe"?

One late June day, a time of year when Muir was still tending sheep and sheepherder nearby, we leave the road near its crossing of the North Fork of the Merced and begin an exploration of the upstream environment closer to his camp. We climb slowly up the steep slope above Bower Cave, brushing through dry, wild oats as high as our heads, passing vigorous post-fire sprouts of interior live oak, all the while carefully skirting back from the ubiquitous clumps of small poison oak, its leaves shiny and green, seemingly announcing its virulency. The seeds of grass and herbs soon impregnate our boots and socks, poking and jabbing our skin beneath the clothing, and we remark to each other how little we differ from a herd of blundering sheep heedlessly dispersing the plants from one place to another. The dry heat, even in mid-morning, is uncomfortable on the sunny, south-facing slope.

High on the ridge, we stop to admire the view across the valley, to the jumble of burned ridges toward the southwest. It is a colorful panorama.

North Fork of the Merced River, near Bower Cave

On the road cuts of dirt tracks probably cleared for logging access, the red earth characteristic of the old weathered soils of the foothill country beat forth in warm arteries of intersecting lines. Like broken bones are the shorter, more narrow, and much straighter gray lines of the upright snags or prone trunks of fire-killed ponderosa pine. The flesh of the view is provided by the yellow-tan of the dried grass and purple-pink swaths of flowering farewell-to-spring. Scattered throughout the tawny ground cover are the dark green freckles of sprouting trees and shrubs. The blue, cloudless sky overarches everything below. While we sit in quiet observation, a red-tailed hawk glides silently by, working the updraft along the warm ridge, his own gazing for a more immediately practical purpose than our own.

Farther along the ridgetop, we struggle through thick stands of manzanita, whose stems reach far above even the tallest grasses, and we begin a descent down the north-facing slope toward the river below. Here the fire apparently burned less hot, leaving the forest more intact. Tall conifers provide broken shade for prospering patches of whitish

Ponderosa pine growing in a carpet of mountain misery

lupine and mountain misery (named for the alleged "misery" of its stain for even a modern launderer), rich with its delicately dissected leaves and white, simple, rose-like flowers. Proceeding slowly down the steep slope, investigating an outcrop of rock where a seep of water cradles flourishing, tiny, yellow monkey flowers and enfolds a shady patch of moss once wet and spongy but now drying in the summer drought, ever avoiding patches of prickly ceanothus and unsettling poison oak (some even beginning to show the red leaves of a distant fall season), we think again of Muir's sheep, his "thousands of busy nibblers," which grazed and browsed these very slopes.

We reach the stream at a place where soaring conifers and massive oaks arch over big leaf maples and white alder, all creating a dense arbor above the dark water as it splashes over smooth boulders and into a long, quiet pool. Tangles of blackberry and elderberry, overspread with rambling vines of clematis, add to the lush coolness. A scattering of orange tiger lilies, planted by nature's graceful hand, and the warble of a nearby house wren add to the illusion of a secluded private garden.

Slowly moving our way upstream, sometimes in the streamside arbor, at other times on the adjacent slope of trees, brush, and grass, we eventually reach a level flat where two stream terraces create a comfortable spot between cool water and steep slope, ideal camping conditions for a band of sheep and tending men. Three massive black oaks rise in solitary grandeur with the usual mix of conifers on both the immediate flat and adjacent slope. Chickarees bound across the ground and from ground to tree trunk; bear droppings suggest other nonhumans visit on occasion. At the head of the level ground, where the valley walls close in tightly, the stream cascades over boulders polished by centuries of rushing water. Just below the rapids, a long, deep pool, bordered by alders and willows, ferns and grape vines, columbine and lilies, sedges and grasses, is permanent home to quiet fish and temporary abode to two human walkers. We wade chest high into the wetness, examining the myriad fringing plants but drawn especially to the bright red roots of the willow that lie in the water. It may not be an "altar rock," but we feel appropriately baptized.

Our day on the North Fork of the Merced is filled with sensations so rich and inviting that we find ourselves unable to make rapid progress upstream. The flowers, never in great masses but constantly present and forever inviting attention, slow us at almost every step—farewell-to-spring, brodiaea, mule ears, everlasting, white yarrow, blue lupine, soap plant, owls clover, milkweed, blue penstemon, monkey flowers (both yellow and pink), pine drops, coral bells, columbine, Mariposa lilies. . . .

If the flowers were not diversion enough, we also find ourselves amid an array of birds, whether sensed by song or by sight: blue-gray gnat-catcher, acorn woodpecker, goldfinch, robin, brown towhee, yellow warbler, black-headed grosbeak, white-breasted nuthatch, Steller's jay, Anna's hummingbird, lazuli bunting, rufous-sided towhee, flycatcher, vireo, red-tailed hawk. Finally, butterflies are everywhere, providing graceful charm and colorful motion, blues and whites, swallowtails and monarchs. We sate our senses, not only by seeing the forms and colors of living creatures but also by feeling the coolness of water and the smoothness of polished rock, listening to wind in trees, smelling the dry earth. Even the mere listing of what we see, quite apart from "study" of character and behavior, commands more time than we have.

We were surprised, frankly, at the richness that we found on the North Fork of the Merced. It is an environment with virtually no visitors, certainly no "tourists." Collectively, the Yosemite-bound crowds miss everything that Muir found in this wild country, and his own words seem as appropriate today as in the last century: "Who could ever guess that so rough a wilderness should yet be so fine, so full of good things."

Muir was lucky to have a full month here, with its endless bountiful nature. But he was also lucky, in one sense, to have the moving band of sheep, because their eventual departure prompted him to discover new places and new natures higher in the mountains. By moving onward and upward, Muir would continue his observations of "fine . . . good things."

4

Discovery

A grand page of mountain manuscript

On the morning of 8 July, Muir and the sheepherding entourage began a move from the North Fork of the Merced "to the high mountains." At least six men, including Billy and "the Don," two dogs, and more than two thousand sheep moved up through the brush of Pilot Peak Ridge, gaining the deep forests of Hazel Green on the ridge's eastern extension that first evening. Over the next week, they moved progressively through Crane Flat, Tamarack Flat, Bluejay Creek, and Yosemite Creek to their next central camp on the upper drainage of the stream descending into Indian Canyon. The transition in environments could not have been more dramatic—from the sweltering heat and dust at 3,000 feet above sea level to the renewing coolness and afternoon thundershowers at 8,000 feet, from desiccated chaparral to verdant forest and meadow, from the lowlands that Muir had learned so well to the "high mountains" in which he would make new discoveries in the solitude of his further explorations.

Bidding fond farewell to the "romantic enchanting beauty and peace of the [North Fork] camp grove," grown through study and admiration to be "part and parcel of [his] mind and body alike," Muir nevertheless eagerly set forth toward the topmost mountains, his constant, avid hunger "to know" and "understand" not only more but "better." His cravings were less easily satiated than the two thousand "flattened paunches" of the sheep, who also "rushed wildly" to their "new pastures."

41

"Eating, walking, resting"—Muir lauds all such simple pleasures as "delightful." But despite "fine spicy plush boughs for bedding" and "a glorious lullaby [of a] cascading creek," he resents "spend[ing] hours so precious in sleep . . . in the midst of eternal beautiful motion, instead of gazing forever, like the stars." Gazing, examining, measuring, sketching, listening, feeling, knowing, understanding—these were the activities coveted by Muir. Sleep, food, clothing—anything that interfered with his independence and freedom to learn and explore—he disdained as an encumbrance.

For Muir, learning was never finished. Even the familiar, observed, measured, and sketched were ever-changing "in size and beauty and number": "Here [at Hazel Green] the sugar pine reaches its fullest development . . . filling every swell and hollow and down-plunging ravine almost to the exclusion of other species." The manzanitas, common since Horseshoe Bend, were "the largest" specimens he had seen; after measuring the diameter of the bole and the overall height of a particular shrub, and composing twenty-nine lines of description and natural history of this "wide-spreading" plant with "clusters of small narrow-throated pink bells" hanging among "pale green glandular [leaves] set on edge by a twist of the petiole," Muir concludes, "I must try to know them better." Toward Crane Flat, the immense height and breadth of red and white fir (forty-eight lines of description), each nearly 7 feet in diameter and 200 feet tall, contribute to their being the most "notable" and "noble" he has seen. Not only unique individuals but also a novel composition are discoveries worthy of marvel: "Three pines, two silver firs, one Douglas spruce, one sequoia—all of them, except the two-leaved pine, colossal trees—are found here together, an assemblage of conifers unrivaled on the globe."

Beyond the flowery meadow of Crane Flat, Muir is elated to find *L. parvum*, "a grand addition to [his] lily acquaintances." He notes variety within the species in size, up to 7 or 8 feet high, and the number of flowers from one to twenty-five, even within the same meadow. He wonders how "man alone and the animals he tames [can] destroy these gardens" when even the "lumbering . . . wallow[ing] bears harm not a one." While he makes "acquaintance" with the lilies, Muir observes that the passing travelers on their way to Yosemite Valley "seem to care but little for the glorious objects about them." To him, "the dullest eye in the world must surely be quickened" by this "tree-lover's paradise."

However infinite the mysteries of the glories of the present to plumb, Muir can never resist the voices he hears to "come higher" and discover the richness and freshness beyond: "What landscapes I shall find

Back-lit branches of a Jeffrey pine

with their new mountains and canyons, forests and gardens, lakes and streams and falls." Nevertheless, rather sedately he remarks, "A fine discovery this," upon hypothesizing the glacial history of Yosemite while observing striations on huge, smooth granite erratics near camp at Tamarack Creek:

> And with what tool were they quarried and carried? On the pavement we find its marks. The most resisting unweathered portion of the surface is scored and striated in a rigidly parallel way, indicating that the region has been overswept by a glacier from the northeastward, grinding down the general mass of the mountains, scouring and polishing, producing a strange, raw, wiped appearance, and dropping whatever boulders it chanced to be carrying at the time it was melted at the close of the Glacial Period.

In fact, his less unequivocal "discovery" of the well-documented "white fragrant Washington lily" leads him to the exuberant, "The whole world seems richer now that I have found this plant in so noble a landscape."

Looking down into Yosemite Valley the same day, Muir perceives "a grand page of mountain manuscript that [he] would gladly give [his] life to be able to read" and "bewail[s] how little we may learn, however hard we try!" His efforts are certainly endless, spending the day "sauntering and seeing, steeping in the mountain influences, sketching, noting, pressing flowers." Even when his investigations leave some questions unanswered, just gazing at the "external beauty" is "enough to keep every fibre of [him] tingling."

The wild adventure of edging out on the cliff to peer over Yosemite Falls is not entirely the singular event that Muir chroniclers portray; he admires the "continuous bouncing, dancing, white bloom" of Cascade Falls as a fair rival to the higher Yosemite. Nor are the roaring waters the only natural objects worthy of attention: He shifts his gaze from the "dizzy precipices" to the streamside rocks underfoot, to sing the praises of the inconspicuous, gray water ouzel (encountered for the first time at the North Fork camp), a "yet finer bloom . . . than the foam-bells in eddying pools." Muir appreciates the delicate bird as much as the raging falls.

Faithfully and attentively recording the lodgepole pines, willows, purple spirea, sedges, daisies, lilies, columbines, buckwheats, oxytheca, and junipers along Yosemite Creek, Muir looks to the new domes in the distance: "What rich excursions one could make in this well-defined basin! Its glacial inscriptions and sculptures, how marvelous they seem, how noble the studies they offer!" For Muir, every new rise, every new bend through the mountains, offers ever more opportunity to discover more about the old, something about the new.

❀❀❀❀❀❀❀❀❀❀❀❀❀❀❀

The vagaries of road relocations and land ownership render the modern climb from Bower's Cave to Crane Flat, from foothill brush to mountain forest, from stifling heat to refreshing coolness, slightly different from Muir's travel. Yet the opportunities to see and experience new natures, to continue the learning, to maintain the discovery, are ever present.

The initial grade onto Pilot's Peak Ridge retains the route of the past century. A dirt road climbs steeply, winding into dry ravines and out onto even-drier ridges, all the while ascending toward the top of the main crest. Chamise chaparral and a pasture of dried grasses yield to open, burned forest and manzanita brush. Billowing dust is raised by each vehicle, but, luckily, there are few. The main interlude to unremitting heat is a short pass through a forested upland valley. A tall canopy of pine and cedar and a lower one of sprawling maple create a bower over a trickle of quiet water bordered by arching chain fern and rose-colored columbine. For drivers on the road, the contrast offered by the site is an invitation to pause and look for what is new. A western tanager chirrups from high on some hidden branch overhead. A gray squirrel lightly bounds over the carpet of fallen needles and cones. Might an orange-flowering lily grace a moist spot by the stream or water-striders skim its still pools?

Once the initial climb is over, the road continues eastward, following the contour and swinging below Pilot Peak with its crowning fire lookout. The elevation gained softens the heat. The forest fire has created a mosaic of snags and brush, with isolated groves of green conifers singing in the breeze. The road rather abruptly encounters more un-burned forest with its welcome shade. Shortly beyond, where it joins a network of Forest Service roads radiating from a recess in the ridge, the route passes by the first flowering dogwood, festooned in early summer with tight clusters of green, corn-kerneled fruit. A little farther, a locked gate and warning signs announce to the traveler that Hazel Green, a private ranch, cannot be explored, forcing a return to the radiating road intersection and a northward retreat on a twisting, oiled surface to the modern Big Oak Flat Road, shortly below its final ascent past the park boundary into Yosemite.

Meadow at Crane Flat

At Crane Flat, we wander through the forests of Muir's "tree lover's paradise." Here, for the first time on our, and Muir's, route, stands the dense, mature forest of pines and true fir, Douglas fir, and (nearby) giant sequoia. Massive, towering, clustered tightly, these trees have rained down a torrent of bark and needles, branches and twigs, trunks and cones, thereby creating a deep and irregular carpet that impedes even our slow, goal-less stroll. We work our way to the edge of the meadow.

More than the forest, the grassy glade presents novelty—new plants, new flowers, new birds, new insects—amid the familiar sensations of past trips. We admire the sight of 6-foot grasses softly swaying in the breeze and of 3-inch dragonflies and 1-inch fritillary butterflies that speckle the sky. Sensations are rich: the joyful warble of the Lincoln's sparrow and the persistent whisper of the leaves of quaking aspen, the redolence of mint in the air, and the soft coolness of spongy wetness beneath our feet. Blossoms abound—cone flowers and cow parsnip, Queen Anne's lace and goldenrods, buckwheats and senecios are all familiar—but a purple mallow along the meadow's edge and a lavender phlox among the boulders seem new to us, at least here. We look closely at a winged insect that frequents the mint flowers—a fly, 1.25 inches long,

46

including feathery feelers, an orangish head with a black longitudinal stripe, black wings ornamented with a couple of yellowish spots, and an intensely iridescent blue body. We make a quick sketch with the hope of identifying it in our field guides at camp.

By moving slowly along the meadow edge, we encounter a patch of burned forest, the opening of blackened and broken snags newly invaded by bracken and numerous young sugar pine, fir, and incense cedar. Newly fledged chipping sparrows perch on a low branch of a burned white fir, an adult busily feeding them. On a fragrant mint plant below the blackened snag we seek a further examination of the unidentified colorful fly and find ourselves peering also at a large honey bee that temporarily shares a flower with the fly. Buzzing constantly from plant to plant across the meadow, the variety of bee species (as many as a dozen) intrigue us, and we promise ourselves to read up on their natural history. The jerky foraging of a house wren up and down a sapling fir, perhaps feasting on the large red ants that flow around the trunk, catches our attention.

At the upper end of the meadow, where an exposure of rounded granite boulders supports a few small black oaks from lower elevations, and a few quaking aspen from high altitudes, we study the work of red ants as they busily move about their caches of twigs and needles carefully aggregated beneath protruding lips of the rock. Nearby, other flowers grace the meadow near the outcrop—monkey flower, orchid, thistles, clovers, aster, and sneezeweed. Within a large patch of lupine, we glimpse a slinking mammal—a fox or an especially wary coyote—that quickly disappears beneath the plant cover, seemingly headed for a grove of pines into that fingers outward from the adjacent forest to the meadow. Looking among the lupine, we find patches of disturbed ground—fine, dry soil exposed as mounds of dust—but no prints of either people or other animals. Broken lupine stems suggest, however, that some bodies have recently moved through. We imagine sharp-canined predators chase chipmunks or dig gophers here, a potential that adds to our sense of future finds at this familiar spot.

In the evening, we walk quietly in search of the meadow's most "famous" (the word is relative) discovery, North America's largest owl, the great gray. Although we have searched casually before, we have never enjoyed a sighting here and the prospect is enticing. Rare throughout California and always few in numbers, great grays are regularly reported by bird enthusiasts in a few mid-elevation meadows of Yosemite, including those at Crane Flat. The evening's excursion brings no sign of large dark wings beating low and long across the grass, and we leave with only a shadowy vision stored for the future.

On an afternoon dark with clouds and a threat of rain, we slide down a roadfill just west of Crane Flat into the lowland of Hazel Green Creek,

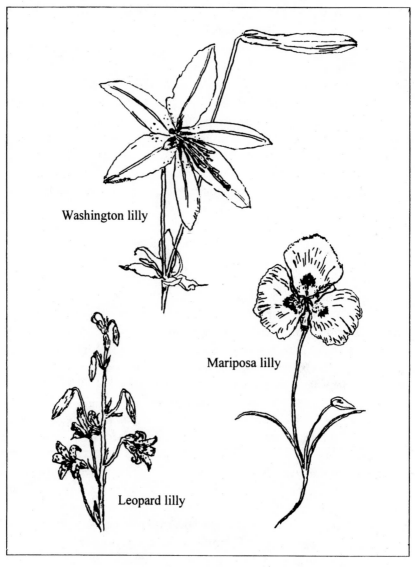

Washington lilly

Mariposa lilly

Leopard lilly

Three lilies, as sketched in the field by Geraldine Vale

searching for the sort of site described by Muir—"a small brook flowing through hazel and dogwood thickets beneath magnificent silver firs and pines." We are not disappointed. Great trees overlook a luxuriant tangle of flowering dogwood, shrubs, ferns, and other herbaceous plants, all centered around a tiny flow of water. Reminded not of the often thirsty Sierran coniferous forests but of the lush, mixed forests of the Pacific Northwest, we make our way over and around the thickets and logs, probing deeper into the cool, moist green. When the heavy drops start to fall, it is even easier to imagine a setting in coastal Oregon. But what brings us back is a flower, the Washington lily, for Muir, "the finest of all the Sierra lilies." In other years, we have seen these giant white lilies only occasionally here and there along the Tioga Road and the road to Glacier Point, and Muir described a few on Tamarack Creek, but here, today, on a rainy July afternoon, we greet dozens. Some are nearly finished flowering, their whiteness faded, their petals drying, but most radiate a glow that brightens the dark forest on that dim day. The rain pours down a deluge by the time we climb back up the roadfill to reach our car.

On afternoons less stormy (and sometimes in early morning calmness), we enjoy walking up the narrow road that leads to the Crane Flat fire lookout. Our search is usually for birds—singing fox sparrows, elusive wrens, and an only-once-sighted pileated woodpecker. We have a favorite spot to look for McGillivray's warblers, a shallow recess (perhaps a byproduct of road construction) luxuriant with elderberry and currant, young fir and alder, walled by towering sugar pine and white fir, in midday full of sun and light, a place seemingly full of secrets. A warbler does not always rise from within the thick tangle with a short burst of song and a flash of color, sable bib and saffron breast against the soft, green leaves, and perhaps is more often missed than encountered, but we always look, hopeful for a renewed discovery. At the road's end, moreover, near the lookout buildings, we once spotted, darting among the blooming manzanita, an Allen's hummingbird, an unusual sighting for Yosemite judging by David Gaines's book on the park's birds.

Birds are usually what we seek, but the shrubs, the manzanita, create a more dependable display. By summer, the small, pendulant, white, urn-shaped flowers are spent, replaced by the neat clusters of fruits that are reminiscent of bunches of tiny green delicious or gravenstein apples; "manzanita" means "little apple" in Spanish. Even more consistently present than the fruits are the buds for next spring's new growth, short arcs of overlapping scales, which hang from the ends of the branches. Muir may have wandered on this very slope when he described them

Cone flower with bumblebee; Washington lily

in great detail and admiration, wondering "how old these curious tree-bushes are, probably as old as the great pines." We look carefully at green fruit, glossy leaves, and peeling red bark. We join Muir in trying "to know them better."

Jeffrey pine, in left-foreground, and sugar pine, in right mid-background, near Gin Flat

Above Crane Flat, the modern road climbs, as did the trail followed by Muir, along the ridge separating the drainages of the Merced and the Tuolumne, through "superb" and "comparatively open" forests, "letting in the sunshine on the brown-needle strewn ground," and beside "charming garden-like meadows." A stretch of the Old Big Oak Flat Road allows access to his next camping place, a small expanse of rounded, granite boulders and shady, moist meadow beside Tamarack Creek.

We discover Muir's description of Tamarack Flat to be still appropriate: "[It is] another fine meadow embosomed in the woods, with a deep, clear stream gliding through it, its banks rounded and beveled with a thatch of dipping sedges. . . . The two-leafed pine [is] common here, especially around the cool margin of the meadow." The "dipping sedges" rounding the banks of the stream, which itself flows "bank-full in the meadow with silent speed," particularly impress us.

We have no similar success in locating, downstream from the Flat, the glacial scratches that prompted Muir's speculation about the work of flowing ice in the sculpture of the Yosemite Sierra. (Perhaps Muir was farther downstream, closer to Yosemite Valley, where a tongue of ice flowed; here we seem to be in unglaciated country.) Our wanderings over the rounded granite exposures along the creek, however, do pro-

Granite boulders on open flat, below Tamarack Flat

duce discoveries of different sorts. The stream still tumbles, as in Muir's day, "rejoicing, exulting, chanting, dancing in white, glowing, irised falls and cascades." Below, on a quiet stretch of water, we happen across a tiny sunny meadow, a stream of water set among patches of green bracken, grasses, sedges, yellow mimulus, blue phacelia, and a grove of small fir. We are attracted by bird calls and soon find ourselves surrounded by the voices and wings of red-breasted nuthatches, mountain chickadees, juncoes, brown creepers, and hermit warblers, all flitting constantly in the fir saplings about our heads. For a while, a junco and creeper play peekaboo with us around a low tree branch. On a high, bouldery mass, firmly rooted in a rock crevice, we find a patch of Dutchman's breeches, for us an unexpectedly dry and sunny spot for this delicate plant. Nearby, on a low, gently rolling expanse of granite, we happen across a group of six grinding pits, worn by generations of earlier visitors to Tamarack.

As we sit beside the pits, feeling the prickling of granite on our bare legs and hearing the songful joy of air sifting through the pines, we watch hikers on the trail below—a group of six young men, hurrying along in loud conversation; a mother and three young children, whose slow stroll nevertheless is not punctuated by frequent pauses to investigate rushing water or flitting birds, flowering plants, or human artifacts; and a dozen other assorted hikers, all similarly intent on getting somewhere down the trail. Discoveries of "Heaven's unquenchable enthusiasm," what so captivated Muir, seem not a part of their experiences.

As much as Tamarack Creek retains the character described by Muir, Yosemite Creek, where he, with sheep and sheepherder Billy, camped for a night, seems different to us today. Instead of coursing "forty-feet wide . . . about four-feet in average depth" with a flow that was "nearly silent," this stretch of Yosemite Creek is far more modest—15 feet across at its widest, 4 feet deep only in the largest pools, and rushing over riffles more than sliding quietly. Our visit after a dry winter explains the varying character. Clearly the less changeable parts of the landscape resemble the impressions of Muir: bordering lodgepole, fringing willow and spirea, flanking "sunny flat of washed gravelly sand" covered by tiny flowering plants, and, rising beyond, "a wavy upsloping plain of solid granite . . . ice-polished . . . like glass [with] shallow hollows [supporting] patches of trees."

We spend a gloriously lonely afternoon sauntering over the "wavy" granite along Bluejay Creek. Tumbling water and rock crystals, lodge-pole rooted in rock cracks that permit only angled and stunted growth,

Yosemite Creek

Steller's jays noisily protesting our presence, pole and rope remnants of a long-ago abandoned shelter—we examine them all, attuned to new discovery as we "faithfully watch and wait" for the "next appearance [that] will be better and maybe more beautiful than the last."

5

Wildness

How fiercely, devoutly wild is Nature

Beginning in mid-July, for three weeks the sheep grazed contentedly without major event, and thus Muir explored untethered from the "blessed silver fir camp" in the upper drainage of Indian Canyon Creek. He wandered widely through the nearby ridges and lowlands, up to the top of Mount Hoffmann and the shores of Tenaya Lake, and down to Yosemite Valley. During these weeks, Muir engaged in what is his most famous mountaineering feat—a face-forward, bare-heels-only hold onto a narrow ledge that allowed him to look over Yosemite Falls. Yet, this incident lasted but an instant of his weeks in the region. Far more common were quiet hours and days watching "daybreak and sunrise," marveling how the rain made "the rock glitter and glow," becoming acquainted with grasshopper and fly, rambling up mountain tops, analyzing meadow origins, and admiring the strength and steadfastness of Sierra juniper. Observation and discovery in the solitude of wild Yosemite continued to be Muir's avocation and preoccupation.

What did "wildness" mean to Muir? How important to him was "wildness" in the Yosemite landscape? How "wild" was the "mountaineer" Muir himself?

Muir little guessed the coming threats to his "Valley of Light" in the twentieth century. Whether it was the log house at Tamarack, which he explicitly saw as a "valuable" aid to future tourism, or the roads that bore travelers to Yosemite, which he seemingly accepted without comment, Muir expressed more regret over visitor attitudes than visitor impacts.

Of gravest concern to him were not the throngs of tourists but rather the flocks of "woolly locusts," which seemed nevertheless at the time "but a feeble band" within the "mighty wilderness." Envisioning their increasing numbers, however, Muir bemoaned their eventual greater destructive powers first on seedlings, then forests, until "only the sky will . . . be safe."

Thrilled with a first clear view of the "noble walls" of the valley from a ridge along the Yosemite Creek drainage, but later frustrated in his attempt to see straight down the vertical cliffs, Muir had one of his "wildest," much publicized experiences. "Cautiously set[ting] his feet" on precarious various viewpoints, he fears the jointed granite will flake off and send him plunging downward "more than three thousand feet," and chides himself not to "go out on the verge again." Yet, "cautious remonstrance is vain," and at the brink of Yosemite Creek's tumble to the valley below, his mouth filled with bitter artemesia leaves "to prevent giddiness," Muir slowly edges barefoot along a narrow 3-inch shelf to the brink to bask in the "tremendous grandeur" of "a perfectly free view down into the heart of the snowy, chanting throng of comet-like streamers." Most accounts end at this climax. But Muir himself notes that his initial "triumphant exhilaration" is "soon followed by dull weariness." He vows thereafter "to keep from such extravagant, nerve-straining places." Nightmares of the whole mountain sheering off into the abyss repeatedly arouse him from sleep. Two days later, "the danger of that adventure" troubles him even more, and his activities return to his more usual ones of "sketching, pressing plants, studying the wonderful topography and the wild animals," usually on the gently sloping, nonthreatening surface of North Dome. "To learn any lesson in the divine manuscript," Muir declares himself "eager to offer self-denial and renunciation with eternal toil."

Although intent on quelling the "wildness" within himself, Muir admires the commingling of wildness and serenity in nature: "How fiercely, devoutly wild is Nature in the midst of her beauty-loving tenderness!—painting lilies, watering them, caressing them with gentle hand, going from flower to flower like a gardener while building rock mountains and cloud mountains full of lightning and rain." Even the wildness of the "lightning and rain" seems more glorious because of its unpredictability in arrival but certainty of swift departure. At the silver fir camp, the vicissitudes of "mountain building"—and razing— of clouds contrasted with what seem previously to have been weeks of mostly dry skies. The rains descend as "a sort of waterfall as imposing as if pouring from rock mountains . . . sublime thunder reverberating among the mountains and canyons—some strokes near, crashing, ring-ing in the tense crisp air with startling keenness." But typically within an hour or so, "How fresh the woods are and calm after the last films of clouds have been wiped from the sky! A few minutes ago every tree was excited, bowing to the roaring storm, waving, swirling, tossing their branches in glorious enthusiasm like worship."

Other journal entries illuminate the juxtaposition of the wild with the gentle. Pondering the difficulty of fully appreciating Yosemite's "grandeur," he asks the reader to see behind the apparent delicate harmony of "rocks and trees and streams" and recognize that the "sheer precipices three thousand feet high," the "waterfalls, five hundred to one or two thousand feet high," the massive mountains and domes, are each in turn subdued by fringes of trees and grass that soften their sharp edges, mighty cliffs that transform their torrents to wisps, dark woods that hide their canyons. Following a "cinnamon" bear "to make the most of [his] opportunity to learn" about the "sturdy mountaineer," Muir's initial self-confidence that the animal "always ran from his bad brother man" turns to respect for this "broad, rusty bundle of ungovernable wildness" that instead of fleeing returns Muir's shouting and hat-swinging with a defiant, fierce stare and "magnificent deliberation" in sauntering slowly away through the meadow. The experience seems heightened for Muir by the bear's "wildness" being "framed like a picture" in a most "flowery glade" of "tall lilies . . . swinging their bells over [the] bear's back, with geraniums, larkspurs, columbines, and daisies brushing against his sides."

Surprisingly, it is not the powerful, "ungovernable" bear, but crea-tures much less imposing that Muir labels the "wildest." At the North Fork of the Merced, it was squirrels, both California gray and Douglas. The appeal seemed to lie in their "fiery, peppery" movements, each one "a hot spark of life, making every tree tingle with his prickly toes, a condensed nugget of fresh mountain vigor and valor." One might attribute such dramatic labeling for this lowly mammal as the result of unfamiliarity with the mightier beasts at these higher elevations, until reading Muir's entry about the even more easily overlooked—by most— common grasshopper as he sketches its "dance" atop North Dome: "Even the bear did not express for me the mountain's wild health and strength and happiness so tellingly as did this comical little hopper. No cloud of care in his day, no winter of discontent in sight. . . . And when at length his sun sets, I fancy he will cuddle down on the forest floor and die like the leaves and flowers, and like them leave no unsightly remains calling for burial." Muir also expresses admiration for the common

housefly, whose wild adaptability allows it "to be everywhere" and whose egg-laying "make[s] all dead flesh fly."

Muir seems to find wildness in himself and the bear, the grasshopper and the housefly, the thunder and the raindrop, massive North Dome and the 8-foot erratic "altar" in the Merced River—perhaps, however romantically, finding in them an independence from care, a perseverance

Fauna of the Yosemite Sierra: coyote, sphinx moth, and sagebrush lizard

in continual renewal, a talent for bringing harmony to change, that he does not see in human society.

❈ ❈ ❈ ❈ ❈ ❈ ❈ ❈ ❈ ❈ ❈ ❈ ❈ ❈ ❈

From the Tioga Road near Porcupine Flat, we leave the pavement by foot in a southward direction, seeking the site of Muir's camp set "in a magnificent silver fir grove at the head of a small stream that flows into Yosemite by way of Indian Canyon." Our route lacks precision; the clues for the location of the spot are few and we know that no one could ever find for certain the site of the three-week camp called "blessed" by Muir. We seek the greater environment, the experience of his location more than an exact relocation.

The mild morning, with white cumulus already "mountain building" in the sky, holds the prospect of a stormy afternoon. The noise of cars on the road is soon left behind as we climb a gentle, sandy slope among the lodgepoles. Leveling off, the forest abuts a wet meadow, rich in the fuchsia splashes of shooting stars and the songful greeting of a drably mottled Lincoln's sparrow, colorful only in melody. Ah, if only the flowers could sing! The narrow stream, with vertical banks held firm by the dense, moist sod, splashes over boulders exposed at the bottom of its deep trench. Tiny blue violets with faces upturned; chipping juncoes, their outer tail feathers flashing white; and less-welcome whining mosquitoes become our companions.

We angle up a steep slope densely forested in red fir. Fallen trees whose prostrate logs are taller than our heads and exposed, rounded boulders, even more massive than the logs and protruding high above the accumulation of tree debris, force our circuitous wandering. Beneath towering trees, a tiny green tree frog hesitates a moment, then somersaults away from our approach.

The slope curves onto a dry, broadly convex ridge, and the dense forest yields to an open stand of Jeffrey pine; occasional fir and western white pine; and patches of chinquapin, manzanita, and huckleberry oak. The granite gently rolls in sheets, in places sheathed in hard, lichen-covered rock, but in others weathered into the coarse sand and pebbles so typical of these midelevation uplands. In the sand of this granite garden are rooted jewel flowers and buckwheats. A mountain bluebird perches on a broken-topped, 15-foot red fir from which it sallies forth to glean small insects and spiders—we are not sure which—from the sandy ground surface. Beyond the small fir and bluebird, a red-tailed hawk soars away southward along the ridge axis, disappearing beneath the growing, gleaming white cloud masses whose darkening bases are beginning to dominate the white and blue. The "sky mountains" also obscure the rock mountain of Half Dome that we could otherwise see from the ridge top.

After following the route of the hawk's flight, we clamber down the far slope, through dense huckleberry oak and increasingly dense stands of fir and pine. Nearing the bottom, we hear the faint song of a stream and see the bright green of meadow plants in a sunny opening. Except for the delicate babble of water, we hear nothing. Suddenly, a sharp "woof" breaks the silence—a brownish ball of fur (we think of Muir's St. Bernard) rolls along the ground away from us and downstream, beyond the trees on the far side of the gentle bottomland, followed by a similarly colored and shaped but much larger sphere. The "broad, rusty bundle of ungovernable wildness" abruptly halts, turns ninety degrees, and, with "magnificent deliberation," stares at us eye-to-eye through the trees. One hundred yards and columns of tree trunks separate us, but we want to be sure that she sees us and does not attack in surprise. We call to her, put on a show of hand waving, while she patiently studies these two intruders. After half a minute or so, she disdainfully lopes after her cub and disappears beyond our sight.

We have seen through the years many bears in Yosemite—less often in the campgrounds in recent years—but none have seemed so wild, so

Clouds building over a granite ridge

bear-like, as this mother and cub. Black bears have apparently increased their range in the Sierra since European settlement, moving down into the lower forests and foothills because the California grizzly no longer lives there, and up into the timberline country because people—and their food—have become summer inhabitants among the subalpine forests and meadows. But here, in the great midelevation forests, we are in the bear's prime natural habitat. It was in this region, in fact, that Muir described most of his encounters with bears, often pursuing the helpless sheep, and we, also intruders in the bruin's domain, are thankful to have seen this mother and young foraging in an isolated meadow, wary of us, wild parts of a wild landscape.

With skies still darkening over the trees, we eat lunch on a boulder amid a grove of red fir on a low terrace above the meadow, ever alert for dark, moving shadows. Cool water, grassy forage, sheltered grove, brushy and tree-covered slopes rising to granite ridges—it was a site such as this that Muir called the silver fir camp. He may have made his bed here, "plushy, sumptuous, and deliciously fragrant, most of it *magnifica* fir plumes . . . with a variety of sweet flowers in the pillow." But if he was camped here, we find no sign of it, nor of anyone else; it is a wilderness free of evidence of humans.

Our return up and over the ridge is in heavy rain. It is appropriate, given the frequent development of afternoon thunderstorms that Muir experienced here: "Grand white cloud mountains and domes created about noon as usual, ridges and ranges of endless variety, as if Nature dearly loved this sort of work, doing it again and again nearly every day with infinite industry, and producing beauty that never palls." A couple of thunder claps boom from above, but we mostly hear the steady tapping of drops on our reluctantly donned ponchos and the occasional splash of our hiking boots in shallow puddles. Atop the open ridge, small rivulets sweep down the granite, carrying needles and cones in miniature debris flows, piling the organics on little flats or behind obstructing rocks. We again think of Muir, writing of wild rains, perhaps on this very ridge: "Now comes the rain, with corresponding extravagant grandeur, covering the ground high and low with a sheet of flowing water, a transparent film fitted like a skin upon the rugged glitter and glow, gathering in the ravines . . . making them shout and boom in reply to the thunder."

By the time we reach the meadow and deep forest below, the downpour has abated. Among the logs and bark of the fir litter we encounter fungi unknown to us, one tall and black and white, another spherical, with points like an ivory-studded mace protruding from the loose, dark duff. (We later search for the species, carefully but unsuccessfully, through several fungus guides; how many discoveries await the student of these lowly but strikingly beautiful organisms, seemingly endless in variety of shape, texture, and color, in Yosemite's reaches!) We find no sign of the tree frog. Water droplets hang from the ends of the dipping lodgepole needles, from the bases of the upturned red fir needles. Their crystalline sparkles in the returning sun rays present a photographic challenge we cannot resist.

Our day's saunter has been in a landscape without people or any evidence of them. Flowers and trees, rocks and streams, insects and birds, tree frog and fungi—wild bears and wild weather—all have been entries on the "divine manuscript" of the "blessed silver fir camp."

The modern trail to North Dome begins on the Tioga Road, a mile or so east of Porcupine Flat. At first, it drops steeply through a dense forest of red fir, following the old access road to a former Park Service camp (en route, crossing the now-abandoned old Tioga Road), and then flattens out among the lodgepole and boulders of the once-bustling Porcupine Creek campground (not to be confused with Porcupine Flat, a small, rather primitive campground upstream). After a boulder hop through the pools harboring wary fingerling trout, we follow the unrolling path beneath shady fir forest, beside several small meadows, and through a

Droplets of rainwater hanging on foliage of a Sierra juniper

saddle where it joins other trails. Here we stop to admire, amid huge rotting logs and broken snags, a wealth of fungus working to return the wood to the soil. One orange-yellow mass, protruding from the decaying flank of a red fir, particularly intrigues us, and we make a note to attempt a later identification. (We are subsequently successful, finding the description of the "chicken in the woods fungus," a reference to its edibility, particularly apt.) The trail continues along a forested slope, then crosses a tiny stream sprinkled with patches of mustard yellow *Senecio*, its golden clusters graced by the orange and black flutter of fritillary butterflies, before climbing steeply onto Indian Ridge. The dry, gravelly upland supports open stands of red fir, which yield to Jeffrey pine as the ridge gradually descends and the rock becomes more massive. Beneath a particularly handsome pine, whose root crawls in the shallow gravel on the surface of the bedrock, searching for drops of moisture, the trail turns off the ridge and plunges down through manzanita and huckleberry oak, pine and white fir, to emerge on a lower domed surface. The towering face of Half Dome looms beyond Tenaya Canyon on the east; the walls of Yosemite Valley grace the south and west. Now crossing shells of exfoliating granite and following a narrow shelf over a vertical cliff (where we carefully choose each footstep to skirt around several washouts in particularly exposed places), the route bottoms out in a level pocket of Jeffrey pine at the north edge of North Dome. It is only an amble up the open granite to the summit.

On a late July afternoon, while we wander over the gently rounded summit of North Dome, we think of the long hours, whole days, that Muir spent here, "thinking . . . studying . . . sketching . . . oftentimes settling down into dumb admiration." At no single small place did Muir spend more time. It was here, in long periods of quiet contemplation, that he was moved to remark about nature being "devoutly wild" amid "her beauty-loving tenderness."

And "wild" it seems to remain today. To the east, a distant wilderness of peaks and canyons fills the view, extending to the crest of the Sierra. Making a great sweep across the foreground—a half mile below our feet and upward a half mile above our heads—rise the great walls of Half Dome and Cloud's Rest, enfolding the wilderness of Tenaya Canyon. Binoculars help us to imagine people, tiny specks, atop Half Dome. By peering over North Dome's edge, we see the single clear evidence of humanity, the switchbacks of the Snow Creek Trail, climbing the near side of the canyon far below. Shifting our gaze to the south, we see the vertical cliff below Glacier Point and Illilouette Canyon (with its headwall waterfall) dominating the near scene, with Mount Starr King

Looking down on North Dome from a higher ridge to the north

beyond, and still farther a wild forest rising gradually to the gentle
sculpture of Buena Vista Crest on the horizon. Flashes created by the
windshield glass and body chrome of cars moving among the trees
along the Glacier Point Road remind us, however, that the wildness
in this direction is more compromised. Turning toward the west, we
look down the great valley, with the dissected south wall on the left
and the massive cliffs near Yosemite Falls on the right. The vertical
slopes end abruptly against the flat floor of forest and meadow, and
here the wildness seems to end, overwhelmed by car-strewn roads,
bicycle-crowded trails, and rigid rows of canvas cabins. Surely Muir
would regret these intrusions to nature's "tenderness," more than the
switchbacking trail or the flashing cars.

Where had Muir sat "thinking" and "studying," we wonder—atop
the flat boulders open to the sun and wind, or perhaps in the shelter
of dwarfed, weather-twisted Jeffrey pines clumped near the summit?
His eyes must have been drawn to the same nearby wildness that drew
ours: thickets of huckleberry oak ringing the gentle summit area; tiny,
dried ferns rooted in roofed crevices of granite; flowering, reddish-pink
penstemon scattered over the undulating rock, itself mostly impervi-
ous to the elements but in places cracked and weathered into isolated
perched boulders like icebergs in a sea of granite. Still other summit

View eastward from the summit of North Dome, toward Half Dome

features that are part of our visual experience, however, were not present in Muir's day, and all are intrusions to the wild—other humans (a German-speaking couple, a single older man, a family with a teenage son), footprints in the gravelly sand, a few fire rings of blackened rocks, and, as always, jet trails overhead in the blue sky. But Muir would have joined the visitors in their fascination with the scurrying golden-mantled ground squirrels, chasing each other through the maze of tree trunks, shrubs, and rocks.

In total, then, how "fiercely" wild is "Nature" as experienced on North Dome today? The initial response must be that it is muted by the crowds of modern visitors to Yosemite. Trails, vehicles, roads, buildings, planes, footprints, even other people dilute the wildness that Muir knew here. And yet that first impression is only partly true. From the fragile, lowly, desiccated ferns hugging the rock crevices to the kingly wall of Half Dome, from ground squirrel and Jeffrey pine to distant forests and peaks, the landscape is still mostly wild. Our solitude is lessened by other humans and their trappings, but the opportunities to learn and discover the "beauty-loving tenderness" of "Nature," even a "fiercely, devoutly wild" nature, remain.

View westward from the summit of North Dome, into Yosemite Valley

Perhaps, we think, wildness here may have even made some gains over the last century. Despite the congestion in the valley below, the meadows that in Muir's time were pastures for milk cows and hay-fields for livestock forage grow wild again, abloom with grasses and flowers and abounding in grazing deer—their green verdure, restored and protected by the park he so passionately promoted, is a welcoming reassurance to our eyes. Above the valley, lightning fires now revitalize the forests, evidenced by the charred stand on the valley rim below North Dome just to the northwest and by the smoke rising from the ridge near Mount Starr King this very afternoon, signs of the relatively recent let-burn policy. Also above the valley floor, the scar from the 1980 rock slide beside Yosemite Falls stands out bold and white in an otherwise gray rock wall (as would, a few years later, at the upper end of the valley, the scar from the great rock slide of 1996). We recall the beginning of the trail that we walked this morning; where Muir knew sheep camp, guns, and dogs, we crossed abandoned roads and a closed campground, the artifacts of asphalt and fire pit being reclaimed by clumps of sedge and logs of red fir. Small concessions to the wild, perhaps, but concessions nonetheless.

Wildness

Before we don our packs to begin the climb back to the Tioga Road, we make a final search for the grasshopper and housefly that so intrigued Muir on North Dome. We had been alert for his "friends" when we first strolled onto the gentle granite slope and remained so as we explored the summit expanse, but we make good contact with neither. Perhaps the brisk, westerly breeze discourages flying insects—the only flies we notice dart rapidly by our heads without alighting. It was, of course, the earthy abundance of the housefly as a world-wide colonizer that Muir celebrated in his writing on North Dome. Neither naturalness nor native endemism was the measure of the housefly's worth. Its success spoke to Muir of the vibrancy of wildness.

Actor Lee Stetson's impersonation of John Muir in the theater on the floor of Yosemite Valley draws us one mild summer evening. We decide to see "The Spirit of John Muir," as opposed to "Conversations with a Tramp," because it promises a presentation of Muir's experiences in nature rather than Muir's conservation thought. We are curious about what activities Stetson chooses to present, a selection that presumably reflects the expectations of a sympathetic audience.

We anticipate a series of stories about wild escapades, the famous

Stream and water ouzel, as sketched in the field by Geraldine Vale

wild-man Muir that forms one of his popular images. We find that we have not misjudged. Muir is trapped by a snowstorm on Mount Shasta; he rides an avalanche down a Yosemite Valley canyon; he rushes out to observe the rock fall generated by an earthquake; he hazards a climb on the winter ice cone at the base of Yosemite Falls; he runs down the talus on the valley side, boulder-hopping over the precisely packed scree. Admittedly, a couple of subtle stories tell of his observing an eerie shadow atop a cloud deck from the top of Half Dome, and his effort to persuade Ralph Waldo Emerson, on the writer's visit to Yosemite, to camp outside and away from his traveling companions. Mention is made of Muir's conviction that glacial action molded the Sierra and his dispute with J. D. Whitney over the formation of Yosemite Valley. A brief comment about Muir's fondness for the commonplace, however, is not illustrated by examples, of which possibilities are endless—Muir's descriptions of water ouzels or red fir, of black ants or black bears, his "radiant resiny sun trees" or the "glory" of *Lilium parvum*. We hear nothing of Muir's "studies," his sketching, his days spent in sitting, "oftentimes settling down into dumb admiration." We think that those in the theater with us, if they have not read thoughtfully what Muir wrote, can only come away with an image of the man as an acrobatic daredevil, eager for the next thrill-generating escapade: to emulate Muir is to seek out the danger in nature and contest it. Nothing could be farther from the essence of Muir. Far more central to his vision, his behavior, his action is "tenderness." The "wildness" that Muir saw in the natural world was the lily "swinging [its] bells" over the back of a bear.

We enjoy Stetson's performance and are even moved emotionally as we leave. But we are happy to be out in the quiet, tender wildness of the cool evening dusk.

6

Solitude

*Out of sight of camp and sheep
and all human mark*

In moving from the North Fork of the Merced to the deep forests and
sunny domes north of Yosemite Valley, Muir traveled into increasingly
remote and wild landscapes. Miners and grazers in the foothills, small
bands of tourists on the Yosemite road at Crane Flat—these human
contacts were mostly left behind as the Delaney sheep herd moved
along the Mono Trail, long a travel route for Native Americans across
the central Sierra.

Muir was delighted when lingering snow at higher elevations necessi-
tated a slower pace, the sheep "nip[ping] and nibbl[ing] as they liked,"
the sheepherder freed from the chores of constant translocation of flock
and camp: "What fine times I shall have sketching, studying plants and
rocks, and scrambling about the brink of the great valley alone, out of
sight and sound of camp!"

Of course, Muir's times "alone" were generally those "saunterings"
and "wild scramblings" between morning and evening meals. In camp
or between camps, he had few spare moments for his beloved gazing, sketching, and studying. Then, his attention was monopolized by
the encumbrances of civilization—herding the "timid, water-fearing"
sheep across streams; fending off marauding bears; ruing his human
dependence on clothing and "a piece of bread." For the tourists who
passed by them on the Yosemite trail "in parties of from three or four to

fifteen or twenty, mounted on mules or small mustang ponies" and who "seem to care little for the glorious objects about them," Muir spares no kind words: "A strange show they made, winding single file through the solemn woods in gaudy attire, scaring the wild creatures, and one might fancy that even the great pines would be disturbed and groan aghast." He further laments the gold mines that "civilized" the Mono Trail, including the building of a few small bridges, but he expresses thanks that "over the greater part of the way scarce a stone or shovelful of earth has been moved." Yet how naively Muir underestimates the future impact of travelers when he casually remarks that a log house at Tamarack Flat "may become valuable as a station in case travel to Yosemite should greatly increase."

It was out of camp that Muir felt close to nature. On a day when the search for a new campsite allowed Muir time to wander freely, he embraced the opportunity for a quiet ramble, "sauntering and seeing . . . sketching, noting, pressing flowers." A few days later, while the band hesitated at Yosemite Creek, Muir "made haste to high ground" to enjoy "the noblest view of the summit peaks [he had] ever yet enjoyed." But the escape to solitude required not even a wild scramble to a distant ridge. In the evening, taking a break from his domestic obligations, Muir sauntered up the meadow at Tamarack about sundown "out of sight of camp and sheep and all human mark, into the deep peace of the

Lukens Lake, near White Wolf

71

solemn old woods, everything glowing with Heaven's unquenchable enthusiasm."

One quarter of a mile from the Tioga Road, at an elevation of about 8,500 feet in the great forest belt of Yosemite, a dry, broad, rounded ridge often receives our visit in the evening hours. The experience is always the same. We stroll over the sand and gravel of weathered granite, interrupted by frequent piles of boulders and occasional sheets of hard rock. Over large areas, the sands are covered with silky carpets of gray foliage, *Lupinus breweri*, which, even in dry years when flowers are few, complement the whitish gray sands. Patches of brushy huckleberry oak and ground-hugging bearberry cluster near some of the boulders. Massive red fir and western white pine are scattered as isolated individuals or small groves, and the evening sunshine, beaming with yellowish light slanting in from the western sky, makes the reddish-brown trunks of the fir and the brownish-red trunks of the pine glow with luminescence. Our usual search for birds is often unremarkable, with a few juncoes or finches typical (although one evening we shared the ridge with a family of white-headed woodpeckers). Occasionally, we scare up a mule deer and, at least once, have noted the spoor of a black bear. We see no one, hear no one, find no "human mark." The silence is intense. It is a ridge common in Yosemite, with nothing unusual, nothing spectacular, nothing "entertaining." It is always "glorious."

Solitude in Yosemite—although typically portrayed as an oxymoron—readily awaits anyone who cares to find it. As in Muir's time, getting away from fellow humans and their trappings need not require a long trek into the backcountry. Wandering away from camp or road, shunning the trails (or at least the more popular ones), the sojourner quickly bids farewell to the bustling, crowded Yosemite and is welcomed into the solitary wildness that Muir knew. We have often taken such strolls scarcely hundreds of yards from the Tioga Road, onto a weathered dome where we found "glorious objects" in a solitude without "human mark"—lone, gnarled Jeffrey pines rooted in narrow fissures, the vanilla scent of their bark sending out heady olfactory invitations; dark fence lizards scurrying for the cover of huckleberry oak and chinquapin; sky-blue mountain bluebirds flycatching from tree branches; mountain quail darting downslope from our approach; and ancient sheets of exfoliated granite weathered into a nobility befitting great age.

Raindrops on leaves of lupine

Mountain ridge, including Mount Hoffmann, as sketched in the field by Geraldine Vale

On one occasion, near Tamarack Flat, we briefly followed a stream and then a forested ridge, eventually emerging onto an open rock face with a commanding view eastward to Half Dome and the summit peaks beyond. We sat for awhile in the late evening light, completely alone amid a granite garden of flowering plants, bright yellow stonecrop

Glacial erratic boulders and glacial polish, after a rainshower, in drainage of Yosemite Creek

and blue penstemon, feathery and inconspicuous jewel flower, while a noisy flock of white-throated swifts chattered and soared overhead. Still another lonely saunter took us from the roadside through a thick stand of red fir, with the usual dense carpet of decaying logs and branches on the forest floor, up a steep, smooth sheet of exposed granite broken by a ribbon of rushing water that paused in small pools before hurtling on its cheerful way. Even the immediacy of road traffic might be ignored for a brief interlude of solitude, a time to wander along a stream, admiring the water cascading over a fallen log into a deep pool, a slaty dipper winging its way just above the frothy spray, the shore festooned with the rosy pinks of onion, spirea, and monkey flowers. A bountiful solitude in Yosemite offers places for continued discoveries, for observing nature's "endless song."

Muir may have relished his days rambling "out of sight of camp," but his nights, whether passed perched atop a granite boulder or nestled in a bed of "spicy plush boughs," ushered in a particular solitude that especially stirred his spirit. At times, Muir envisioned himself lying on "an altar," his eyes lifted heavenward toward "the stars peering through the leaf-roof," his soul, too, raised in prayer: "Precious night, precious day to abide in me forever. Thanks be to God for this immortal gift."

Solitude

Yosemite nights still can be so. We often walk at dusk, sometimes up a slope or along a trail, but usually on a campground access road, keeping eyes and ears alert for late-arriving fellow campers. As one veil of nature enfolds familiar sights within deep shadows, another is lifted to uncover the mystery of night. A log lying across the darkness of the forest floor becomes a prowling bear. Trees lose first their individual identities, then their collective presence as physical objects become, simply, darkness. The bright canvas of flowers in a meadow gradually fades, the tinkling notes of a tiny stream float into the freed space above the sod. The last loud call notes of the robin yield to the soft flutter of bats swooping low over our heads. Occasionally, coyotes howl in choruses from some distant forest opening. High overhead, the "evening star"—the planet Venus—appearing before the last glow of sun fades away, is lost within the show of tiny lights in the moonless black dome.

We sometimes encounter other walkers in the quiet. We may exchange barely audible signs of greeting, lest the special quality of silence be lost, but otherwise everyone who wanders in the darkening hours seems content to retain a certain separateness, to preserve a personal solitude.

The return to the campground too often breaks the magic of those walks. RV generators hum, dogs bark, people shout, and, especially, music blares, in a multitude of languages and styles: English and Spanish, rock, country, big band, Indian chanting. Not always, but even once seems an affront.

Muir felt similarly frustrated with those visitors who seemed not to appreciate the beauty of unadulterated nature. He could not convince the sheepherder, Billy, to walk to the edge of Yosemite Valley to see the rock walls and waterfalls. "What . . . is Yosemite but a canyon—a lot of rocks—a hole in the ground—a place dangerous about falling into—a d--d good place to keep away from," reacted Billy. Muir, who observed that the sheepherder was "apparently deaf to all stone sermons," gently mused that Billy's insensitivity to the "precious . . . gift" rendered him "hard to place in this wilderness," that is, a visitor inappropriate for Yosemite. The heavy visitation to Yosemite—in recent years exceeding four million tourists a year—unquestionably diminishes the opportunity for solitude, but more important than their numbers is the attitude of the many drawn by the beauty of the spectacle but insensitive to the true nature of that beauty. Lack of respect is the fundamental threat to solitude in "this hospitable, Godful wilderness."

7

All Things, All Scales

Gazing into the face of a
daisy . . . or . . . afar over domes and peaks

For a week at the end of July, Muir turned his attention away from
the ridges and valleys near Indian Canyon Creek to two more distant
features in the Yosemite landscape. From the "silver fir camp," he spent
a day rambling to the summit of Mount Hoffmann, and, on the next
day, he was "up and away to Lake Tenaya." For the rest of the week, he
reflected on these saunters.

🌲🌲🌲🌲🌲🌲🌲🌲🌲🌲🌲🌲🌲🌲🌲🌲🌲🌲🌲

That Muir believed "the sculpture of the landscape is as striking in
its main lines as in its lavish richness of detail" is well illustrated as
he wound his way to the 11,000-foot summit of Mount Hoffmann.
Through his keen observations of both the massive and the minuscule,
he anticipates the thrill of discovery. "Come higher," he imagines nature
to beckon "wooingly," and follows "tremulously" in the hopes of knowledge of a "new realm of wonders," from the vast view of distant new
mountains to the closer study of "new plants, new animals, [and] new
crystals": "From garden to garden, ridge to ridge, I drifted enchanted,
now on my knees gazing into the face of a daisy, now climbing again
and again among the purple and azure flowers of the hemlocks, now
down into the treasuries of the snow, or gazing afar over domes and
peaks, lakes, and woods, and the billowy glaciated fields of the upper
Tuolumne."

Buds and flower of a fleabane (daisy)

Muir makes no specific mention of reaching the summit—only commenting that it is "the highest point in life's journey [his] feet have yet touched"—but he describes the watersheds, geology, and landforms one would view from it. "Who wouldn't be a mountaineer!" he exclaims; yet what seems to excite and satisfy the "tingling palate" of his body and soul is not just the destination but the whole journey along the way. In his study of the three trees new to him on the lower slopes—"hemlock (*Tsuga mertensiana*) [mountain hemlock], . . . mountain pine (*Pinus monticola*) [western white pine], and the dwarf pine (*Pinus albicaulis*) [whitebark pine]"—he is certainly interested in the general forms, the "delicate, sensitive, swaying branchlets" of the hemlocks, the 4- to 6-inch cones and large 5- to 6-foot diameters of the western white pine, and the dwarfing of the whitebark pine at timberline "so completely . . . that one may walk over the top of a bed of it as over snow-pressed chaparral." But when his passion for the hemlock ("the most beautiful conifer I have ever seen") sends him high and deep into its branches, it is not the sight of the far view or the caress of the strong wind that "makes [his] flesh tingle." It is the "touch of the flowers [immature cones]," and he "revels" at the "wonderful wealth of color . . . the dark rich purple" of the pistillate cones, the "almost translucent, blue" staminate cones. Back on the ground, "so dull and forbidding at first sight," he discerns "radiance in some places . . . so great as to be fairly dazzling"

Muir sketch of Mount Hoffmann. John Muir papers, Holt-Atherton Department of Special Collections, University of the Pacific Libraries. Copyright © 1984 Muir-Hanna Trust.

as he identifies the "shine and sparkle" of individual crystals of "micas, hornblende, feldspar, quartz, tourmaline."

One must be receptive to varying scales, whether of size or time or beauty or wildness, lest "we in our timid ignorance and unbelief" see only a "howling desert." Indeed, the mere act of juxtaposition often heightens our appreciation: "The broad gray summit is barren and desolate-looking in general views, wasted by ages of gnawing storms; but looking at the surface in detail one finds it covered by thousands and millions of charming plants with leaves and flowers so small they form no mass of color visible at a distance of a few hundred yards." For Muir, one extreme almost anticipates the other: "the more savage and chilly and storm-chafed the mountains, the finer the flow on their faces and the finer the plants they bear."

Rather than boast of the rigor of his walk up Mount Hoffmann, Muir, unlike many of today's mountaineers, speaks of it as a "ramble," finding "wild excitement" running *down* the ridge and ravines to camp. More like a modern tourist, he finds a soaring eagle "striking" and is especially drawn to the small mammals—a marmot "unfortunate" in being caught by his dog, Carlo, and a pika busily cutting and amassing little haystacks of "lupines and other plants" to store underground for the long season of snow.

The next day, on Muir's descent to Lake Tenaya, natural wonders at various levels await his discovery, as he virtually immerses himself in the immediate and descends into the sublime. Wading through "starry parnassia bogs" and "gardens shoulder deep in larkspur and lilies, grasses and rushes," he travels "down a broad majestic stairway into the ice-sculptured lake-basin," where he traverses "a wondrous breadth of shining granite pavement . . . for the first time."

As usual, Muir devotes the majority of lines in this section of his journal to observations of the vegetation. From the broader perspective, he identifies and classifies three "kinds" of meadows—in wet basins, in dry basins, and on ridge and mountain slopes—and describes their probable origins and species compositions. From the smaller perspective, he does not end before exclaiming, "what fine painting and tinting there is on the glumes and pales [tiny reproductive parts of grasses], stamens and feathery pistils." Discussing the red fir, he looks up to marvel at the descending concentric circles of the groves "so trim and tasteful . . . one would fancy they must have been placed in position by some master gardener," then lowers his eyes to admire the carpet of small roses and buckwheats before declaring the scene a "charming pleasure ground." Whether trees are 5 inches or 5 feet in diameter, crucial to understanding these "hardy mountaineer[s]" is an examination of their tiny, fraction-of-an-inch flowers, the pistillates, "mostly hidden in the leaf-tassels" of the lodgepole pine, the staminate "rich" and "showy" only to the eyes of a sensitive beholder. In "studying" the red fir, he first comments on their "gigantic size"—"measured one near two hundred and forty feet high, the tallest I have yet seen"—then two pages later reflects on the cones for a full page of text, finding their form, size, and color "grand" but the small scales, bracts, seed wings, and seeds inside, "if possible . . . more beautiful than the outside . . . tinted with the loveliest rosy purple with a bright lustrous iridescence . . . [and with] dark brown."

Finding in "no Sierra landscape . . . anything truly dead or dull," Muir discovers interest in even the ants and mosquitoes, the borers and the gallflies, focusing on behavior, but not failing to record the 1 inch of the mosquito "from tip of sting to tip of folded wing," and the 1.5 inches of the borer's ovipositor, "polished and straight like a needle." Although no bears lumber through this chapter, Muir, like modern tourists, finds delight in following the antics of the much less formidable and much smaller rodents—chipmunks and marmots—remarking of the former that "few of the Sierra animals interest me more; they are so able, gentle, confiding, and beautiful, they take one's heart, and get themselves adopted as darlings." Behavior is his focus here also, as it is with the birds—flickers, robins, mountain quail, blue grouse, and Clark's nutcracker (which he was unable to name but shrewdly observed with adequate detail for our identification: "a curious dove-colored bird that seems half woodpecker, half magpie or crow. It screams something like a crow, but flies like a woodpecker."). Curiously, however, throughout the entire journal he does not mention the larger avifauna of Yosemite—the raven, the owls, the hawks—save for the one reference to an eagle in this chapter. In the case of birds, at least, could smallness be not just as enticing as largeness, but perhaps more enticing? Maybe so, for a man who writes so eloquently of "the history of a single raindrop" rather than of the development of a major thunderstorm.

❋❋❋❋❋❋❋❋❋❋❋❋❋❋

The alignment of the Tioga Road from Porcupine Creek to Tenaya Lake, arguably the most spectacular section of this spectacular road, generally follows much of the route followed by Muir on his walks to Mount Hoffmann and Tenaya Lake. Close to the pavement, the modern visitor can still discover what Muir observed: groves of mountain hemlock, graced by hanging clusters of "dark rich purple pistillate" cones, on the old road to the May Lake parking area; "wondrous breadth[s] of shining granite pavement" west of Tenaya and along the lake's north shore; "gigantic" red fir with tiny cone scales "tinted with the loveliest rosy purple" near Porcupine Creek; shoulder high "larkspur and lilies, grasses and rushes" among peaceful meadows and beside dancing streams, such as Hoffmann Creek or Snow Creek; "charming pleasuring grounds" of tiny flowers, including sulphur yellow buckwheats and pink, furry pussy paws on sandy flats and slopes, even on the roadcuts themselves; and multitudes of chipmunks and numerous marmots, which "take the hearts" of today's visitors at Olmsted Point.

We particularly revel in the meadows, such as Snow Flat, still a "delightfully smooth, level sod," where we enjoy morning strolls beneath the imposing fortress of Mount Hoffmann. On one morning walk, from a standing perspective, we think the meadow lacks flowers, but by looking carefully, even squatting down, we find tiny yellow mimulus and shiny buttercups, a few purple gentians and tall Queen Anne's lace, isolated fleabanes and a colony of shooting stars (both past their prime), and, backlit by the sun, the bright, delicate lacy flowers of the many grasses. By lying down and scanning the "smooth level sod" from the level of the feathery grass blooms, we see the surface alive with dancing bodies of dark dragonflies and orange fritillary butterflies, of brown skippers and blue coppers, of flies and other insects whose names we do not know. We wonder what still tinier life abounds here, too small to see,

Exfoliation sheets on granite slope, west of Olmsted Point

amid the dragonflies and grasses, and recall Muir's words: "When we think of the small creatures that are visible, we are led to think of many that are smaller still and lead us on and on into infinite mystery." Our microscopic revery is short-lived, however, broken by the macroscopic call of a Clark's nutcracker, and we twist our heads to see the bird flying just above the tops of the tallest lodgepole, its beating wings audible from our prone perch, its departure framed by the turrets high on the flank of Mount Hoffmann.

All of this wildness awaits discovery in the solitude of the roadside, and yet the cars drone by with people eager "to get on the trail," to climb the rocks, or to swim the lake. We admit a certain admiration for the occupants of the Winnebagos and buses that hesitate at Olmsted Point—at least they observe both the grand vistas of Tenaya and Half Dome, as well as the closer ones of marmot and nutcracker, of rock polish and glacial erratic.

To climb Mount Hoffmann requires no special skills or talents, no ropes or pitons, no unusual stamina or endurance. It is a steep walk, with an ascent of 2,000 feet in 3 or 4 miles, with only the last scramble close to being a trial for the faint of heart. Its greatest challenge is a test of patience, not personal mettle. We, like Muir, find the walk "glorious."

The modern trail to Mount Hoffmann leaves a small parking lot, a wide place on the old Tioga Road, where red fir tower over small, dark-watered ponds. First passing by granite boulders (where numerous large snags house hungry, noisy offspring being fed insects by solicitous adult sapsuckers) and forested groves (where grouse or quail are frequently flushed from the undergrowth), it then climbs a short, steep, sunny slope to the moraine-dammed May Lake on the mountain's eastern flank. The High Sierra Camp, a cluster of white canvas tent cabins, sits quietly on the shore with a view of the still, sapphire surface and the massive, turreted bulk of Mount Hoffmann beyond.

The trail is peopled with an intermittent but constant flow of day-walkers and overnighters, backpackers and camp guests, old and young, men and women. A half dozen camping parties scatter beneath the trees along the lake's western shore, but beyond them the human stream dries up. We will meet only twenty or so people on our long day on Mount Hoffmann.

We admire the mountain hemlock that border the lake on its north-west bank, perhaps where Muir first encountered the species. The grace-fully slender and drooping branches, downturned top, and blue-green needles make the tree one of our favorites, particularly because it typically grows in groves on moist, sheltered slopes and recesses at high elevations. We do not, as Muir did, "gladly . . . climb . . . the first tree" we find, but nonetheless enjoy the feel of the cool, soft needles in our fingers, much as Muir savored "the touch of the flowers." No Sierran conifer offers a more pleasing combination of sensual enticements.

The trail above May Lake is only an informal route pounded out by decades of repetition of human bootfalls, sometimes a worn path, sometimes a faint track of trampled plants, sometimes an unmarked scramble over boulders. It turns from the shore and climbs through willow thickets bordering a stream singing over the indomitable angular rocks of metamorphosed limestone. Bright yellow flashes in the green foliage catch our attention, and we soon enjoy, eye to eye, two Wilson's warblers, easily identified by their jet black caps. They dart about tirelessly in the open twigs of the willow, occasionally flitting to the low branches of nearby hemlock, foraging for insects that they glean from the plants. Later in the day, we will find three twenty-fourish walkers— two men and a woman—also keeping company with these warblers. The males, who share a single pair of binoculars, pay most attention to the birds, and we overhear a conversation about earlier avian encounters:

"Have you seen the hooded warbler out East?"

A doubtful mumble.

With much enthusiasm, "They're bad ass!"

The woman, wired into a Walkman, with the audible beat of rap music extending beyond her ear plugs, seems oblivious to both bright bird and water song that charms the place. She reminds us of Billy, whom Muir quotes as uninterested in Yosemite, where "there is nothing worth seeing . . . only rocks. . . . You can't humbug me."

Beyond the thickets and a moist, rock-dotted meadow, we climb through open groves of western white pine before gradually emerging onto the alpine upper flank of the mountain. Prostrate whitebark pine now scatter over the sandy slope, replacing the larger and more upright form of these trees a little lower down. The loose sand and gravel slides down with each climbing step upward, making for slow walking, but the ever-grander vistas of distant domes and rugged ridges are incentives enough to move us slowly along. We agree with Muir's exuberance over these views of "glorious congregations of peaks. . . . Who wouldn't be a mountaineer!"

As the steep climb levels out on a sloping bench, we search the gray and white gravels for tiny alpine plants. We find in flower a small, ground-hugging pea and a low, yellow buckwheat. The "beds of azure daisies . . . ivesia, penstemon, orthocarpus, and patches of *Primula suf-*

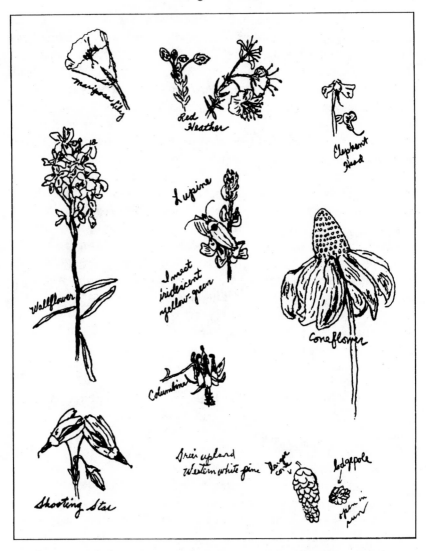

Flora of the Yosemite Sierra, as sketched in the field by Geraldine Vale

fruticosa" that Muir so admired on the mountain's "broad gray summit" are not in sight. Still, the clusters of blooms, best appreciated by a close inspection gained by a stoop or squat, float in the sea of bright rock crystals in which they find root, making a showy Lilliputian world.

The extremes in scale strike us. Here, with the grandest of sweeping vistas, is also the magnificence of the smallest of flowering plants. Neither scale detracts from the other; at lower elevations, by contrast, the more proliferous trees and shrubs distract the eye from smaller plants while they also obscure the far-flung view. Here, both the vast and the minute, the majestic and the subtle, coexist in visual harmony.

Two hundred feet below the summit, where the gravel bench abuts the slope of massive slabs of granite that rise to the top of Mount Hoffmann, and where the northwest face of the mountain falls a thousand vertical feet to the headwaters of Yosemite Creek, we stop for lunch. Free of the time constraints that preoccupied us here a few years earlier—concern for lighting necessary to click the shutter for a comparison photograph for a different book—we revel in the leisure to take in food for body and spirit.

It is easy to imagine Carlo, Muir's St. Bernard companion, catching and killing a marmot on Mount Hoffmann, so free of fear are they. We idly discourage two from sharing our lunch, while we share their rock table, nestled in one of Muir's "devil's slides" between the towered buttresses on the mountain. Our protective diligence need be only periodic, however, as we find the always hungry rodents nosing the ink pen and notepad in the open pocket of our pack as much as they investigate the gaping bag of sandwich, nectarines, and pecan cookies. Between the quick waves of an arm that are necessary to secure possession of our food, we find our eyes carried to a junco industriously pecking—we do not know at what—in the snow bank overhanging the vertical cliff, and to a pair of deer, as tiny as alpine buckwheats, beside one of the lakes far below. Beyond the lakes and deer rolls the open, tree-speckled granite, and beyond the exposed rock sweep the dense forests that extend into the hazy foothills.

Turning our heads, we gaze over, as did Muir, the "axis of the range in [its] robes of snow and light." We could imagine no scene more grand. Yet we notice only one of the twenty visitors that day stopping to admire reflectively this particular panoramic sweep of mountains and canyons, so intent are they all in "reaching the top" to enjoy the single view from there. Muir must have stood, and probably sat for a while, on the highest point, but he makes no mention of it, so little importance did he ascribe to the finale of the climb. We, too, climb the granite slabs toward the summit but find ourselves not needing this time a footstep on the small flat above which there is only sky. A few feet below the top, we turn around and clamber back down the granite ledges.

The clouds have been building rapidly since midday, mushrooming in billowy masses ever higher in the deep blue sky. Each echoes the smooth, convex domes of white granite far below. By mid-afternoon, their bases are darkening, but none mimic those in the headwaters of

View from the summit of Mount Hoffmann, to the northeast, with the headwall of a glacial cirque in the left foreground

Indian Creek, alternately obscuring then revealing the view like a veiled dancer. Here, the bright light on nature's stage remains undimmed.

While recrossing the sun-drenched bench below the summrnit, we watch a large buteo hawk—perhaps an eagle, and if so, maybe a distant relation to the one that Muir observed here—ride the spiraling updraft, and we listen to rock wrens whistling on the open boulders, but not until we begin the steep descent down the loose sands and gravels do we encounter some late afternoon hikers climbing up the mountain. We are asked repeatedly, "Is it worth it?" and "Is it better than here?" Others inquire, "How far is it?" or "How long?" A precocious four- or five-year-old, hiking with her grandfather, speaks for most of those we encounter on Hoffmann. She chats with us entirely centered on her concern for *time* by announcing, "We've climbed quite a bit already, and we may not make it; it's 3:15 already, and we have to start down at 4:30." Too few of our fellow walkers seem to linger anywhere along the way or at the top. The goal seems to be to rush to the summit, click a quick photograph, and race back down.

Still lower, we enter the open stands of western white and upright whitebark pines, where we are reacquainted with bright yellow

View from the summit of Mount Hoffmann, to the southeast, toward the crest of the Sierra Nevada

wallflowers and purple whorled penstemons, now both glowing in the late light. Below in the meadow, a corn lily blooming creamy white— it escaped our attention on the way up—prompts us to wonder why, among all of those plants, only one is in flower. The Wilson's warblers are still flitting about the willows, the water still merrily surging down the rocks. We slowly pass beside the quiet surface of May Lake and then down the formal trail, heavy with upbound backpackers headed for the High Sierra Camp, to the towering red fir and small, black ponds guarding the parking lot.

Our times at Tenaya Lake have been varied. Childhood memories include camping (once fending off an afternoon bear from a camp table's food) and picnicking beside the gently lapping waters. In recent years, we have climbed the rock slope on the northeast corner, strolled the east-end beach, and wandered the west-side shoreline to rephotograph scenes originally taken at the turn of the century. We have seen the lake in many moods: the quiet stillness of clear mornings with a mirror-like surface; the breezy afternoons when whitecaps sweep across from west to east and billowy clouds climb over Tenaya Peak; a cold, late spring day when easterly winds reminded us of winter; a noon hailstorm that whitened the ground and closed the road; another stormy day when the lake domes gave birth to roaring cascades and waterfalls; and a summer

Tenaya Lake, from Olmsted Point

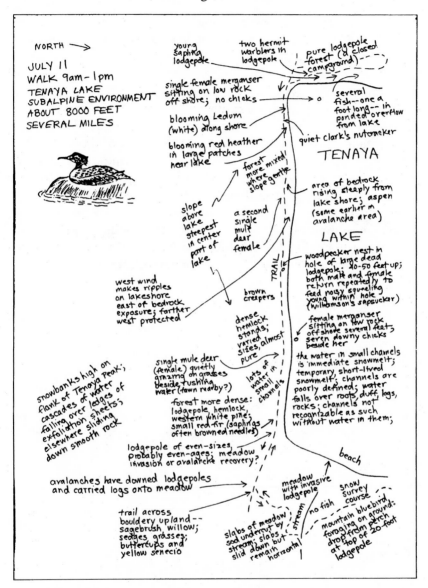

Page from journal of Thomas Vale. A walk along the south shore of Tenaya Lake.

afternoon when, though the sun was shining at the lake, an intensely black thunderstorm obscured the distant peaks at Mount Conness. We usually notice California gulls patrolling the north shore; bright pink penstemons tucked between the rocks of the road cuts; stately, massively trunked Sierra junipers rooted in cracks of the gleaming glacial polish;

and lizards rustling among the dried leaves beneath manzanita and huckleberry oak. Tenaya never fails to impress those who admire both grand scenes and intimate views.

One morning walk along the south shore greeted us with birds and flowers, trees and mammals, wind and waves, rushing water and shining granite. We observed familiar wild friends and discovered new acquaintances, both animate and inanimate, both large and small, in the solitude of a Tenaya wilderness within earshot of the Tioga Road. We encountered only a single man perched admiring the view from a boulder at the lake's west end, and a couple eating lunch on a waterside rock at the middle of the south shore, but all three were quiet, seemingly content to be in the midst of wildness. The windsurfers were mere blurs of color near the far shore along the road. More disruptive of the mood of the wild, more in violation of Muir's vision of nature's "vast show . . . of divine symbols," was the shouting of the rock climbers from across the lake.

8

Rational Romanticism

The natural and common is more truly marvelous and mysterious than the so-called supernatural

For three days in early August, Muir focused on a "strange experience," revealing his thoughts on "the supernatural." An overnight trip to Yosemite Valley interrupted his several weeks at "the silver fir camp" on the upper drainage of Indian Canyon Creek. The incident emphasizes his commitment to natural history.

Sprinkled throughout Muir's journal entries in *My First Summer* are references to Shakespeare, Emerson, Shelley—and a single, rather obscure one to Nathaniel Hawthorne. So unlike that oftentimes gloomy, brooding, guilt-ridden descendant of Puritan persecutors of Salem "witches," haunted by the evil alongside the good in all of us, was John Muir. Whereas Hawthorne found darkness in the forest, Muir found light. Whereas Hawthorne was quite comfortable with the supernatural, Muir preferred the "natural." But also how like Hawthorne was Muir in his relentless pursuit of the "truth," of understanding the relationship between people and nature, of resolving the conflicting obligations to individual self and to larger community. Hawthorne's stories are largely allegories, often with a message about the promise of freedom in nature—whether for Hester Prynne and the Reverend Dimmesdale in the forest or for Giovanni Guscanti and Beatrice Rappaccini in her

father's garden—being illusory: Solitude in nature can be only temporary; it is the fate and the duty of humankind to return at last to society
and to answer to its laws or change them. When Muir descends from
his wilderness to the relatively civilized society of Yosemite Valley, his
solitude broken, he exhibits a little of both conformity and resistance to
human society.

Muir titles this, his sole chapter on Yosemite Valley, "A Strange
Experience." Yet his reactions to this "one well-defined marvel of [his]
life of the kind called supernatural" confirm him to be not the Mystical
Missionary as so many of today's interpreters portray him, but, rather,
a "Rational" Romantic who finds such "spirit-rappings . . . comparatively useless and infinitely less wonderful than Nature's open, harmonious, songful, sunny, everyday beauty."

As he describes the incident, having sketched all day atop North
Dome until late afternoon, "trying to draw every tree and every line and
feature of the rocks," Muir's typical empirical studies were interrupted
by a sudden premonition that his former University of Wisconsin professor, J. D. Butler, was in the valley below. Although he had received a
letter from the professor the month before about a visit "some time in the
summer," Muir, intent on an entire summer surrounded by the "wilderness," had previously concluded that he "had not the slightest hope" of
seeing Butler and dismissed from his mind all possibility of a meeting. At

Half Dome from Olmsted Point

first, Muir feels "drawn irresistibly" to find his way down to the valley that afternoon, through the dense growth of trees and brush despite the late hour, but rather than yield to his "strange, telepathic" vision, he is instead won over by his "common sense," reasoning daylight would be long gone by the time of his arrival. Contrary to his common depiction as a maverick in matters of fashion, he labels himself as "desperately bashful and shy," and gives his lack of a coat as one reason for his initial hesitation to arrive at the hotel after dark. True, he must "drag" himself from the temptation and "never for a moment wavers . . . in [his] determination to go down to him next morning," yet he proceeds with remarkable practicality, restraint, and planning when faced with his "transcendental revelation." The next morning, he carefully dons "a clean pair of overalls, a cashmere shirt, and a sort of jacket—the best [his] camp wardrobe afforded." Even then, he further reveals his acute awareness of the conventional when he writes that the guests at "the gloomy hotel" had "all stared at [him] in silent wonderment, as if [he] had been dropping down through the trees from the clouds, mostly [he supposed], on account of [his] strange garb."

A Romantic he was, nevertheless. Having surprised his friend on the Vernal Falls trail, Muir joins Butler to show delight in their reunion by "quoting the poets," while "ever and anon gazing at the stupendous rocks about [them], . . . growing indistinct in the gloaming." Dinner conversation resounds with lines from Shakespeare. Later, at rest, Muir describes his sleep as "strange . . . in a paltry hotel chamber after the spacious magnificence and luxury of the starry sky and silver fir grove." He pities his more worldly friend, "compelled to dwell with lowland care and dust and din, where Nature is covered and her voice smothered, while the poor, insignificant wanderer enjoys the freedom and glory of God's wilderness."

And missionary he is as well, but finding his God not in the mystical but in nature's "everyday beauty." Although he makes no comment about the intruder he passes by in the valley "making hay on one of the meadows," he has a sharp tongue for those visitors that he observes to be "so little influenced by [Yosemite's] novel grandeur, as if their eyes were bandaged and their ears stopped." He laments that most of them "were looking down as if wholly unconscious of anything going on about them, while the sublime rocks were trembling with the tones of the mighty chanting congregation of waters gathered from all the mountains round about, making music that might draw angels out of heaven." His admonition earlier to his dog, Carlo, "that he must be careful not to kill anything" (after Muir is unable to revive "an unfortunate woodchuck" rescued from his dog's capture) is reiterated strongly about sports fishermen, lacking sensitivity to their companions in nature:

> Yet respectable-looking, even wise-looking people were fixing bits of worms on bent pieces of wire to catch trout. Sport they call it. Should church-goers try to pass the time fishing in baptismal fonts while dull sermons were being preached, the so-called sport might not be so bad; but to play in the Yosemite temple, seeking pleasure in the pain of fishes struggling for their lives, while God himself is preaching his sublimest water and stone sermons!

A philosopher too, Muir repeatedly returns to contemplate the un- usual nature of the Butler incident, and by the end of the day's entry, back at camp, he concludes that "it seems supernatural, but only because it is not understood. Anyhow, it seems silly to make so much of it, while the natural and common is more truly marvelous and mysterious than the so-called supernatural. . . . The worst apparent effect of these mysterious odd things is blindness to all that is divinely common."

Blindness to the "divinely common" was not a fate suffered by Muir. Having had only eight days the previous spring to roam the valley, he used this opportunity to explore his "new world," including the "regular gradations" of the golden-cup oak from the chaparral-like form at camp to the fully developed "wide-spreading, gnarled, picturesque trees" on the talus slopes below. He paints a word picture of the roaring descent of the Merced River through Vernal and Nevada Falls so lucidly and luminously that, had he read them, Albert Bierstadt could have spared his own trip to their cascades.

The last two days' entries from camp show any sixth sense to be a phenomenon of the past: The men are surprised at night by marauding bears who kill several sheep. Muir regrets that the forays to retrieve the scattered flock have interrupted his studies, but seems partially consoled by the lessons he has learned about "these noble bears."

Muir had written the evening of his return from the valley, "Haw- thorne, I fancy, could weave one of his weird romances out of this little telepathic episode, the one strange marvel of my life, probably replacing my good old Professor by an attractive woman." Little did Muir guess his more "Rational" Romanticism would someday stand at least equal with, perhaps in brilliant challenge to, that master of gloom.

On a visit to Yosemite in the middle 1950s, a boy, eleven or twelve years old, discovers a popular booklet on the coniferous trees of Yosemite National Park. The details of the discovery have been lost to time. Does he notice the guide on a bookshelf of the museum? Had the leaflet been purchased by his parents on a vacation trip? The motivation that prompted it has been similarly clouded by the passing years. Is his sensitivity to the subject of the booklet inspired by a project assigned by his science teacher, an encouraging word from his parents, or the enkindling consequence of a campfire talk by a Park Service ranger-naturalist? However it happened, though, the event cascades consequences into the future. The Yosemite landscape had already become a special place for the boy, an environment of happy vacation days with his family, and, partly because of that association, it had been developing into a revered ideal, a Romantic vision of perfection. With the discovery of the booklet on conifers, however, begins the weaving of rational threads into the tapestry of that vision, the warp of Romanticism strengthened with each passage of the shuttle by the weft of Rationalism.

The boy learns to recognize the common trees in the lower elevations of Yosemite—ponderosa pine and incense cedar, white fir and Douglas fir—and appreciates the habitat preferences of each species. Bark characteristics, length and geometry of needles, general tree form—all allow him to identify most trees even while scanning the rapidly passing forest from the backseat of the family car. On the valley floor, however, he struggles in vain to distinguish young white fir from young Douglas fir, the saplings of both trees indistinguishably orderly in branching form and lacy in needle character. At higher elevations, still other trees emerge as particular species from the generalized forest: Long branches graced by pendulous cones distinguish sugar pine; the delicate symmetry of short, upturned needles and whorled branching identify red fir; clusters of long needles on the ends of branches and vanilla-smelling bark mark Jeffrey pine. His family stops to camp at Tuolumne, where the mostly monotypic forests allow ready identification of lodgepole pine, and the boy wonders if the needle-miner moth, which infects these trees, might allow the spread of the more elegant mountain hemlock, with its dense foliage of short, blue-green needles and pendulous branches—a naive thought given the hemlock's need for much more moist soils than the pine. On the flank of Mount Dana, where the boy climbs with his parents and sisters, the five-needled whitebark pine, festooned by clusters of purple cones, sprawls prostrate over the angular, reddish boulders.

Discovery of the conifers is followed by unearthing other hidden treasures—the broadleaf trees, the mammals, the reptiles and amphib-

Rational Romanticism

LODGEPOLE PINE
Pinus contorta var. latifolia Engelm.

Lodgepole pines are an exception to the general rule that the forested areas of Yosemite consist of numerous species with one kind predominating. However, in many localities in Yosemite, especially in filled-in river or lake bottoms at higher elevations, lodgepole pines form extensive pure stands. At elevations of from 8500 feet to timberline Sierra junipers, mountain hemlocks, and whitebark pines frequently associate with the lodgepoles.

Practically all of the conifers in the park are restricted in distribution to certain quite characteristic elevations. This is also true with the lodgepole pines to a large extent. They are high mountain trees preferring elevations between 7000 and 10,000 feet. However, they are found both above and below this belt, occasionally quite abundantly, but more frequently sparsely scattered along the water courses. In Yosemite Valley at an elevation of 4000 feet, many typical specimens occur along the Merced River near Yosemite Lodge and Camp 19. The Glacier Point road passes through a fine lodgepole pine forest in the meadows on both sides of Bridalveil Creek.

This species conforms so strictly to the generalized pine type as to be

Cone and foliage of lodgepole pine. (Inch squares on background)

Page from the booklet "The Cone-bearing Trees of Yosemite National Park." James E. Cole, 1939, *Yosemite Nature Notes* (Special Number), 18(5), p. 21.

Yosemite Falls, framed by an arching branch of black oak

ians, the glacial forms of the rocks, the causes of winter snow and summer thunderstorms. Later will come the birds and flowers, the shrubs and streamflows. Each new understanding helps to structure the boy's rational interpretation of this romanticized landscape, the knowledge enhancing the perfection, the ideal encouraging the learning.

Long after, as an adult and with his spouse, he will study in the Yosemite landscape, researching and writing on meadow dynamics and landscape change. He will describe the importance of past events, former incidents blurred or even erased by time, that help to form the present. Some observers will still look upon such events as "pure chance," as mechanisms that have no causes but which generate effects, as happenings that have no rational explanation. He will resist such mystical interpretations, preferring to say, simply, that the causes are not clear, perhaps even unknowable, but that they nonetheless existed; it is only the obscuring of evidence over time that makes the explanation problematic. Muir was right: "The natural and common is more truly marvelous and mysterious than the so-called supernatural. . . . It seems supernatural, but only because it is not understood."

The man thinks back to his first childhood encounter with the booklet on Yosemite conifers, an experience that helped to form his subsequent life and carry him along in the current of love and study among the meadows and domes of the high country. He tries to articulate in his mind what happened and why, but he cannot. Unknowable but not supernatural, the past event lies in the shadowy distance of the past.

On an unusually mild, mid-summer afternoon in the valley, we wander along a quiet stretch of the Merced River, absorbed by the wind rippling the surface water, tossing the heads of meadow grasses, and high overhead waving the sun-burnished clusters of ponderosa pine needles. Our eyes rise higher still, up the great vertical walls, towering above the flat valley floor. As much as we study the smaller scale of water and grass and tree, we never entirely lose sight of the larger framework of the great valley's rectangular geometry.

It is a form that marks history. In 1865, California's state geologist, Josiah Whitney, published a scientific explanation of the origin of Yosemite Valley. The vertical walls and flat floor, he reasoned, resemble the classic shapes produced when faults allow the downward fall of a block of the earth; Yosemite Valley, then, was created when the floor dropped in a cataclysmic event, "the wreck of matter and crush of . . . worlds." Not quite a supernatural genesis, but close.

Black oak, ponderosa pine, and wall of Cathedral Rocks, Yosemite Valley

A few years later, Muir would challenge this interpretation. As an alternative, he invoked the work of "winter daisies," ice crystals massed into great glaciers, which slowly and gradually created "the noble walls . . . [and] the level bottom . . . dressed like a garden." To Muir, the appeal of such a birth lay with its noncatastrophic character, its relative gentleness, its consistency with a natural world filled with "harmonious, songful, sunny everyday beauty," its invocation of "the natural and common"—however poetically expressed.

Muir, though he exaggerated the magnitude of glacial action in the Sierra, was nevertheless more right than Whitney, but the great amateur naturalist would, with today's knowledge, embrace more than he did the importance of catastrophic events as molders of the natural world. From the distant extinction of the dinosaurs (whose mortality seems linked to an asteroid impact with earth) to the recent eruption of Mount Pinatubo in the Philippines (whose outpourings of ash and gases reduced air temperatures worldwide), the contemporary evidence suggests that the "harmony" of nature includes the unusual, albeit rational, event. Perhaps more familiarly, the recognition of wildfire and flood as parts of the natural world, including Yosemite Valley, prompts a reinterpretation of what was once viewed as an agent of singular catastrophe as a regular facet of natural systems. The "uncommon," in effect, has become "natural."

Muir, who appreciated the importance of such events in parts of the natural world, would have no trouble in accepting this modern worldview, and he could walk comfortably amid the charred snags on the valley floor. His gaze would be drawn downward to the sprouting fronds of bracken and the scattered seedlings of ponderosa pine, as well as upward to the blackened bark of fir—perhaps made animate by the flash of the white-headed woodpecker on the otherwise ebony snag—and beyond to the vertical cliffs. Muir's faith in the rationality of the natural world and his conviction that it was, at once, both "marvelous and mysterious," were as uncompromising as Yosemite granite.

9

Brotherhood

*More and more in a place like this, we feel
ourselves part of wild Nature, kin to everything*

As it is for so many modern visitors to the summer Sierra, the month
of August was Muir's time in the Tuolumne high country. Leaving the
silver fir camp in the drainage of Indian Canyon Creek, the entourage
of browsing sheep, herding dogs, and tending men moved past Tenaya
Lake and through Tuolumne Meadows to a new camp, the last for
the year, north of the Soda Springs on a "typical glacial meadow . . .
bounded by walls of the arrowy two-leaved pines." For four weeks
Muir's home, this camp allowed him to wander widely into the alpine
country farther north, over Mono Pass and into Mono Basin, and up
to the summits of Mount Dana and Cathedral Peak. Still, the camp
meadow itself was special: Muir described it as "perfect." He spent
three of his four weeks on the "flowery carpeted mountain hall" and in
its surrounding lodgepole forest.

Writing about his experiences at Mount Hoffmann and Lake Tenaya,
Muir penned his since oft-quoted lines: "When we try to pick out
anything by itself, we find it hitched to everything else in the universe."
Out of context, the sentiment may appear simply and purely an early
concept of the web of life, of ecosystem. Yet, when considered along
with the sentence following it, the words take on an anthropocentric
tone: "One fancies a heart like our own must be beating in every crystal

100

and cell, and we feel like stopping to speak to the plants and animals as friendly mountaineers."

Evidence of his very humanistic vision of nature runs throughout the journal. Personifications abound: Nature itself is a poet, a mother (as "wisely, sternly and tenderly she loves and looks after her children"); trees and flowers are brave mountaineers. Storms gnaw at ridges; grasshoppers dance sermons. Muir bids goodnight to the bears, the flies, the grasshoppers; the robin, a "fellow wanderer," reassures him in solemn walks, "Fear not! Fear not!" Viewing even the tiny pikas as "endowed with brain stuff something like our own," Muir seems better able to learn the "lessons they teach . . . to widen [his] sympathy."

Muir expresses the closest brotherhood to the landscapes of the Tuolumne high country, where he would "like to live . . . always." The more "kindly familiar" he becomes with the forests, the lakes, the meadows, and the streams, the more he "should like to dwell with them forever."

Superlatives abound in these chapters. The region is "the most spacious and delightful high pleasure-ground I have yet seen." He writes of their glacier-meadow camping area, "Of all Nature's flowery carpeted mountain halls none can be finer." For the Yosemite range in general he finds no equal:

View southward through Tioga Pass to Kuna Crest

Probably more free sunshine falls on this majestic range than on any other in the world I've ever seen or heard of. It has the brightest weather, brightest glacier-polished rocks, the greatest abundance of irised spray from its glorious waterfalls, the brightest forests of silver firs and silver pines, more starshine, moon-shine, and perhaps more crystal-shine than any other mountain chain, and its countless mirror lakes, having more light poured into them, glow and spangle most.

He wonders if any range of similar elevation has "weather so fine, and so openly kind and hospitable and approachable."

Even should he live in his "Range of Light" eternally, his pleasure, it seems, would depend not upon merely passively becoming "part and parcel" of this perfect natural scene, as did Emerson's, but upon discovering "a new heaven and a new earth every day," for nature is "ever changing," and upon observing and learning new "lessons" of unity and interrelations of all the features of the landscape, whether revealed in general views, from such new wild places as Bloody Canyon, or "by parting the meadow grass here and there and looking down into the underworld of mosses and liverworts." Muir desires nothing more than to continue his "usual" days of roaming widely, "observing, sketching, taking notes." He sees in the fine landscape an opportunity "to study mountain sculpture and soil making," "to study the fine trees," to "study . . . glacial action in mountain-making."

Muir's vision of his ideal life in this "universe in full communion with everything good" did not necessarily include other humans. On a walk to Cathedral Peak, he exclaims, "How delightful it is to be alone here!" He feels "not a trace of loneliness" during Mr. Delaney's week-long absence from the camp. Far from the tourists at lower elevations, he seems even more elated with his solitude: "The whole wilderness seems to be alive and familiar, full of humanity. The very stones seem talkative, sympathetic, brotherly." Neither does he welcome other intruders he views as unnatural. He yearns for a day when he will have "money enough" to escape the work that keeps him in constant view of the "harm" done by the sheep, "outrageously foreign and out of place in these nature gardens." These intruders are not part of the brotherhood. Muir waxes most aggressive when defending his meadow turf from these "hoofed locusts": "Were bears much more numerous and destructive, the sheep would be kept away altogether." When he writes of his dreams to return someday to explore Yosemite further, for which he would "make any sacrifice to try to read its lessons," he pictures himself restrained in no mean classroom, but "walking where [he] like[s] in pure wildness."

In recounting his sidetrip through Mono Pass to Bloody Canyon and Mono Lake, promised by Delaney to be "the wildest of all the Sierra passes," Muir himself questions his attitude toward other humans, in this case a band of Indians he encounters traveling from Mono to Yosemite, whom in lifestyle he proclaims as "not a whit more natural . . . than we civilized whites": "How glad I was to get away from the gray, grim crowd. . . . Yet it seems sad to feel such desperate repulsion from one's fellow beings. . . . To prefer the society of squirrels and wood-chucks to that of our own species must surely be unnatural." Committed to being "natural" himself, Muir endeavors to so extend his concept of brotherhood to the Indians by quoting Burns: " 'It's coming yet, for a'that, that man to man, the warld o'er, shall brothers be for a'that.' " He tells himself, "Perhaps if I knew them [the Indians] better, I should like them better."

In solitude at the head of the canyon after nightfall, having long "lingered" to "examine" the glaciated rocks, the avalanche paths ("How glad I should be if free to pursue such studies!"), a species of dwarf willow (with "not a single stem or branch more than three inches high"), and many carpets of flowers, Muir lies in a hollow on a bed of pine tassels and "recall[s] the lessons of the day." With the face of the full moon above seemingly "filled with eager concern" for him alone, Muir feels "indeed . . . near to Nature." His "wild excursion" continues the next day ("Who could imagine beauty so fine in so savage a place?") as he scrambles through "tremendous walls of red slate savagely hacked and scarred and apparently ready to fall in avalanches." Muir describes in his usual lavish detail the tiny gardens "in all sorts of nooks and hollows," the high falls above him "apparently coming direct from the sky," and the tall Mono Craters "rising abruptly out of the desert" beyond him. Muir "greatly enjoyed the gray east side" of the mountains, whether stooping to study through a lens "the fine striae" of the glacial rocks that indicate the direction of ice flow or peering across several miles to ponder the 2,500-foot-high volcanic cones.

"Glad to get back to the green side of the mountains" several days later, Muir, unlike Delaney, seems to find his beloved Tuolumne land-scape every bit as enticing for exploration as Bloody Canyon. Neither is lacking in solitude or wildness. "How interesting everything is," he proclaims upon his return. On a climb to Cathedral Peak, he exclaims "How delightful it is to be alone here. How wild everything is—wild as the sky and as pure!" And discovery may be paramount. During

Summit of Lembert Dome, Tuolumne Meadows, and Cathedral Peak

the weeks since leaving the foothills behind, Muir had unsuccessfully sought sight of cassiope, or white heather, a white-flowering member of the heath family: "And lo, here at last in front of the Cathedral is blessed cassiope, ringing her thousands of sweet-toned bells, the sweetest church music I ever enjoyed."

Surfeited with knowledge, discovery, solitude, and wildness, Muir lingers with the towering spire above, the tiny blossoms below, "listening, admiring, until late in the afternoon." Muir will return many times to his Range of Light, yet perhaps never again could he give himself over so completely to nature as on "this big, divine day" on Cathedral Peak.

Drawn by the map's hint of large meadows on Dingley Creek, one of which might be that of Muir's camp in the "mountain hall" which he called "perfect," we wander from Soda Springs on the formal trail that parallels the Tuolumne River. The heavily used path is dusty and deep, strewn with old and recent horse and mule manure. The busy foot-traffic on this morning is not exceptional.

The hikers present varied garb—some are clothed in regular "street" tennis shoes and shorts, but most are adorned in an array of the latest gear; fanny packs are obviously "in" this year, canteens "out," losing favor to "slurpy bottles" or simply plastic bottles of name-brand, foreign-produced, exotic-sounding water. An impressive amount of adjusting of straps and weight goes on both in the parking lot near the stable and at the trail head beside the springs, as the mountaineers head out at a 45 degree angle. A father and son ahead of us sport the most incredible assortment of large and small packs and stuff-bags of various recognizable name brands that we have ever seen, all garlanded across their back sides like ornaments on an over-decorated Christmas tree. Most groups chatter happily among themselves, briefly greeting passersby with a nod or hello, but no "It was worth it's"—apparently a comment reserved for climbing tall peaks, not following flowing streams. Only one couple shows any obvious interest in the wonders at their feet—a middle-aged man points out asters, blooming onions, and yarrow to his female companion, stopping several times beside the trail. No one stops to investigate carefully the open forest of lodgepole pine, the occasional western wood pewee perched on a low branch, or, beneath the trees, the granite boulders—dropped by ancient glaciers—with crystals sparkling in the bright sun.

Turning off on a side trail toward Young Lakes, we lose most of our accompanying people traffic, but not until we leave the rutted trail completely, following cross-country up Dingley Creek, are we finally free of human and horse companionship. We will see no one and find no evidence of other people until we rejoin a trail late in the afternoon.

A few minutes beside a channel of water falling over boulders, bordered by an open, sunny forest of large lodgepole, both live sentries and fallen warriors, we find the stream matching Muir's description, singing "merrily down over shelving rock ledges," and we are hopeful that the camp meadow is nearby. But the glories of the stream distract us from the search. The creek flows swiftly, alternately spreading out to paint a glistening red apron across the paler dry rock expanse, and then cascading across sharp but wide declines to pools of various hues of orange, red, and green. A particularly tall fall plunges into a pool 15 feet deep and half again as wide. A buff-colored tree frog in a shallow, pebbly stretch leaps to escape us, sliding down the current helplessly on its back for a time until it rights itself and leaps off on its way. We stop to photograph a pine with a green skirt of bright green and springy moss forming its own island within the breadth of the stream. In another spot, hanging gardens of yellow mimulus spread 30 feet across an expanse of sheltered granite where a seep of water slides toward the creek's main flow. Perhaps the most impressive waterfall, 15 feet in breadth, spills over the flank of a 50-foot fissure down which the stream has cut a straight, vertical-walled cleft. We decide this might be our "perfect" stream.

Higher in the drainage, the environment becomes more meadowy, and we look for characteristics that Muir described for his "finely finished" meadow. Gentians are frequent, as are most of the other flowers he so admired—blue penstemon, red heather, yellow *Potentilla*, rose-colored *Pedicularis*. But the banks of the stream course, itself much narrower than Muir's "three-feet wide," are clothed in flowers and low woody plants, not "rounded by the down-curving mossy sod." Lacking the level surface described by Muir, the meadow rolls gently in the downstream direction. No views of Mount Dana or other panoramas described by Muir are here imaginable, even without the thickets of invasive lodgepole pine. We continue our search, moving farther upstream.

Along a pebbly reach of the streambed, the reds, oranges, and greens of flowers and foliage are joined by blacks and grays as the water slides and splashes over small rocks. From a thicket formed by two 6-foot lodgepoles—one dead—rooted side by side and flanked by an edging of grasses, a mule deer fawn scrambles up from beneath our feet and, on wobbly legs, struggles toward the cover of the nearby trees. In the headwater reach, where open, wet meadow surrounds shallow ponds, two mature mule deer are confused by our approach, darting first one way, then another. Maybe not Muir's meadow, but it is close to "perfect." We peer into the quiet water and find the wriggling bodies of tadpoles, certainly some of them tree frogs, perhaps others yellow-legged frogs. From the forest beyond the soggy meadow, we hear a sound like crashing thunder, though we see only a few clouds, followed by a dull, powerful, sharp explosion. A tree has fallen, and we rush ahead in hopes of seeing the dust and debris rising and settling, as Muir was able to do during an earthquake in the valley.

Even though this meadow is likely one Muir might describe as "beautiful beyond telling," it is not his "perfection." We wander on through the forest, cross an upland, and descend into the drainage of Delaney Creek. Breaking out of the trees, we know immediately that our search has ended:

> I emerged upon a smooth meadow full of sunshine like a lake of light, about a mile and a half long, a quarter to half a mile wide, and bounded by tall arrowy pines. The sod, like that of all the glacier meadows hereabouts, is made of silky agrostis and calamagrostis chiefly; their panicles of purple flowers and purple stems, exceedingly light and airy,

Delaney Creek and meadow, north of Lembert Dome

seem to float above the green plush of leaves like a thin misty cloud, while the sod is brightened by several species of gentian, potentilla, ivesia, orthocarpus, and their corresponding bees and butterflies.

Clouds have rapidly exploded during the last hours, and thunder rumbles from the darkened sky over the now visible Mount Dana. A few drops of rain fall. Ignoring the storm, we wander up the meadow, admiring the flowers and smooth sod, the large deep pools and wall of lodgepole, the sky of cloud and energy. We wade the stream and circle back. Downstream, where the water "sings merrily down over shelving rock ledges," we find a patch of blooming white heather growing below its usual alpine haunts. It is fitting to discover, tucked back in a recess in the rock where it is cooled by the merry song in Muir's perfect meadow, along a creek named for his *First Summer* benefactor, Muir's "favorite" plant, cassiope. He did not mention finding it here, and we could imagine the working of "ever-changing" nature making this perfection even more perfect.

Like Muir, we treasure nothing more than our "huge day[s], sauntering and seeing, steeping in the mountain influences, sketching, noting . . . grand page[s] of mountain manuscript." Over the last two decades our

Flowers and foliage of white heather on granite boulder

research and writing have taken us throughout Yosemite, especially in the high country, and for one of us these twenty years have been atop the two previous decades of childhood and youth when Tuolumne Meadows was a sacred place for wild solitude. We have climbed the peaks of Muir's *First Summer*, Mount Dana and Cathedral Peak; we have wandered on "the north rim of the valley" of the Tuolumne and among some of "the peaks around the highest source of the Tuolumne and Merced"; we have walked over Mono Pass and down Bloody Canyon; we have explored the shore of Mono Lake and the flanks (and a summit or two) of Mono Craters. Over the decades, we have also wandered in places not visited by Muir in 1869 (although certainly frequented by him in subsequent years), including the Tuolumne Canyon below the meadows and the valleys and slopes beyond Tioga Pass.

One place, the Gaylor Lakes basin, always has been special. A recent visit, the first in more than a decade (during which time obligations of research and writing allowed little time to visit old haunts), was like greeting a friend of former times. Moreover, it was not only the broad vista of blue lakes and alpine meadows, the frame of red ridge, white cirque, and green forest, that seemed familiar but also a variety of sensations that were stored in the recesses of our minds, unknown until the place brought them back: the taste of cool wetness and the

Brotherhood

Gaylor Lakes from the crest of Sierra Nevada, looking southward

sound of gentle dripping, splashed into mental image by the sight of concrete foundation blocks for a long-vanished water tank; the feel on bare face and arms of the westerly wind sweeping across the open water; the sounds of boots on gravel in the narrow path beside the lake and of shallow waves lapping on the boulders along the shore; the sight of tufts of red heather emerging from the rocks.

Yet for all that is familiar, the place is also new. Families of mountain bluebirds gliding from tree top to alpine sedge and of water pipits peering quietly from boulders and grasses are not part of the childhood memories. Neither are yellow sulphur butterflies, tiny alpine willows, a coyote striding across the lower basin, and an obsidian arrowhead lying among rounded pebbles. "A new heaven and a new earth every day" seems not only possible but inevitable, even here in a place familiar enough to send back a fifty-plus adult to preteenage years, walking with parents and sisters.

This power of new observation, of discovery, transforms the solitude of other wild places into "new heavens" if they are seen with the mind of the rational romantic. As illustration, we offer two journal pages of our recent wanderings, both amid "the highest source of the Tuolumne and Merced" but otherwise not specific as to location, lest the place names distract from the places themselves.

109

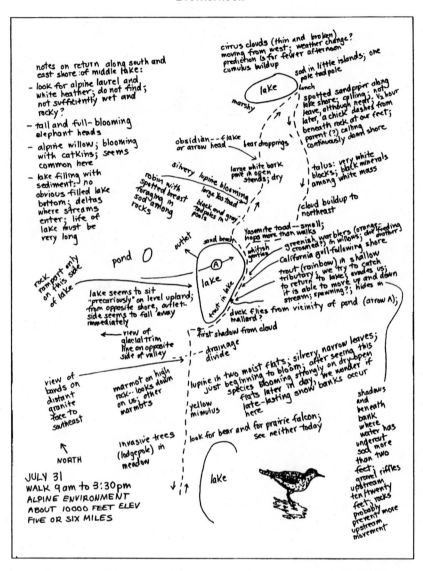

A page from the journal of Thomas Vale. A walk in an alpine environment.

We find ourselves each year increasingly "kindly familiar" with the "fellow mountaineers" of Tuolumne, with whom we "should like to dwell . . . forever." Proclaiming "favorites" implies other phenomena are less desirable, less good, less kindred. Thus we hesitate to be too lavish in our use of such modifiers in describing natural features. If Din-

Brotherhood

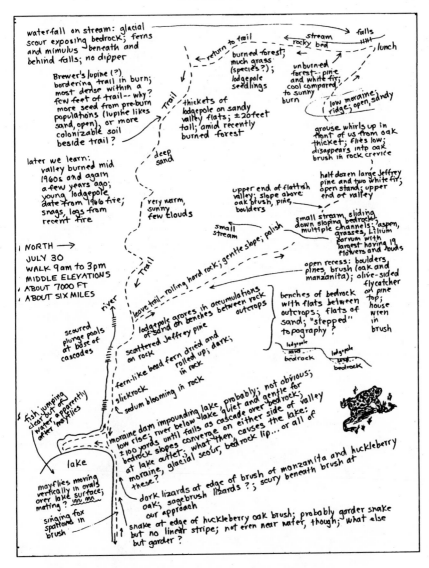

waterfall on stream: glacial scour exposing bedrock; ferns and mimulus beneath and behind falls; no dipper

← return to trail

burned forest; much grass (species?); lodgepole seedlings

→ trail

stream ← rocky bed

falls

→ / lunch

unburned forest—pine and white fir; cool compared to sunny burn

Brewer's lupine (?) bordering trail in burn; most dense within a few feet of trail-- why? more seed from pre-burn populations (lupine likes sand, open), or more colonizable soil beside trail?

Trail

thickets of lodgepole on sandy valley flats; ±20 feet tall; amid recently burned forest

low moraine; ridge; open, sandy

grouse whirls up in front of us from oak thicket; flies low; disappears into oak brush in rock crevice

deep sand

later we learn: valley burned mid 1960s and again a few years ago; young lodgepole date from 1966 fire; snags, logs from recent fire

very warm, sunny few clouds

upper end of flattish valley; slope above oak brush, pine, boulders

half dozen large Jeffrey pine and two white fir; open stand; upper end of valley

small stream

gentle slope; polish

small stream, sliding down sloping bedrock; multiple channels; aspen, grasses, Lilium parvum with largest having 19 flowers and buds

NORTH →
JULY 30
WALK 9am to 3pm
MIDDLE ELEVATIONS
ABOUT 7000 FT
ABOUT SIX MILES

Trail

leave trail--rolling hard rock; gentle slope; polish

open recess: boulders, pines, brush (oak and manzanita); olive-sided flycatcher on pine top; house wren in brush

river

lodgepole groves in accumulations of sand on benches between rock outcrops

benches of bedrock with flats between outcrops; flats of sand; "stepped" topography?

scoured plunge pools at base of cascades

scattered Jeffrey pine on rock

fern-like bead fern dried and rolled up; dark; in rock

lodgepole

lodgepole

bedrock

bedrock

fish jumping clear out of water; apparently after mayflies

slickrock

sedum blooming in rock

moraine dam impounding lake, probably; not obvious; lake quiet and gentle for low rise; river below lake as cascade over bedrock; valley ±100 yards until falls converge on either side of the lake; bedrock slopes; then causes the lake: at lake outlet, what, glacial scour, bedrock lip... or all of moraine, these?

lake

mayflies moving vertically in ovals over lake surface; mating? ♫♪♬

singing fox sparrows in brush

dark lizards at edge of brush or manzanita and huckleberry oak; sagebrush lizards?; scury beneath brush at our approach

snake at edge of huckleberry oak brush; probably garder snake but no linear stripe; not even near water, though; what else but garder?

A page from the journal of Thomas Vale. A walk in a river canyon.

gley Creek strikes us in superlatives, so have other Yosemite streams—Tamarack, Yosemite, Hoffmann, the Tuolumne, the Merced. Beyond Yosemite, we have thought at times still other streams to be deserving of such adoration: the Kings, the Yellowstone and Firehole, the Lochsa, the Umpqua, the Colorado. So too with lakes: Tenaya had, for Muir, "the finest shore scenery," and, while not quarreling with the praise, we

have found ourselves thinking that other lakes are also the "finest"—
Gaylor in Yosemite, Yellowstone in Wyoming, Stanley in Idaho, Crater in
Oregon, Louise in British Columbia. Also with mountains: If Cathedral
Peak was Muir's favorite as a young man in 1869, Mount Dana, so
elegantly positioned, so friendly to climb, so generous in view, was the
best of peaks to a child whose love of the Yosemite high country took
seed and blossomed in the middle of this century. But what of Half Dome
and Mount Whitney, Shasta and Rainier? And meadows: Muir's camp
on Delaney Creek? Why not Crane Flat or Tuolumne or the subalpine
gardens at Tioga Pass? Or Hayden Valley in Yellowstone or the rolling
alpine country near Guanella Pass in Colorado? We have not yet seen the
streams and lakes, the mountains and meadows, in Alaska, the Andes,
the European Alps, or the Himalayas. Muir was right in proclaiming,
"How interesting everything is! Every rock, mountain, stream, plant,
lake, lawn, forest, garden, bird, beast, insect. . . . It seems too great and
good to be true."

Nature's family knows not boundaries of parks, states, countries,
or oceans. We can find brothers in unexpected places if we say, like
Muir, "perhaps if I get to know them better." So we appreciate the
proclamations of friends who cherish the mountains of southwestern

Tuolumne Meadows, looking eastward toward Lembert Dome, Mount Dana,
Mount Gibbs, and Kuna Crest

Colorado, the Yellowstone Plateau, the northern Rockies of Montana, and the wild lands of Alaska. But our own hearts and mountain brethren beckon elsewhere. For us, with our own individual backgrounds and experiences, Muir was right: the Yosemite Sierra is, and always will be, the "finest."

Although our final reflections on Muir's month in the Tuolumne high country convinced us that brotherhood was a stronger theme, our first readings of these latter days impressed us with his sense of stewardship, his desire to protect, as a consequence of his strong feeling of bonding with the landscape that he described as "the most . . . delightful high pleasure ground I have yet seen." His distress over the impacts of the grazing sheep seems symbolic of his later concern over human intrusions more generally into this "pleasure ground": "To let sheep trample so divinely fine a place seems barbarous." It was not until the urgings of Jeanne Carr and Ralph Waldo Emerson that Muir would come to acknowledge that personal kinship or brotherhood with nature was not enough for him and that a stance of public advocacy or stewardship was the logical, and necessary, extension of the feeling of fraternity. Author Frederick Turner suggests that this change in Muir, to abandon the personal life of an explorer and adopt the public life of an advocate, was conscious, and a sacrifice deserving the label of hero.

Unlike Muir, our own involvements with Yosemite, from early encounters to current visits, reflect more the sense of stewardship than of brotherhood. We are drawn to plant and animal, rock and water, sky and earth, past and present, out of a conviction that here is a place that is "divinely fine" more than that here are "fellow mountaineers." Our sentiment underlies the regret we feel over what has happened to Yosemite, not simply the burgeoning crowds of visitors and the ecological impacts they have had, but the growing casual, detached attitude that too many of those visitors bring to this special place, an attitude that sees Yosemite as little more than a cheap place to camp and party unrestrained, an amusement park in which to ride bicycles or climb rocks, to float in a lake or river, to hike fast and far, to toss Frisbees or footballs. What Muir found in Yosemite is still there, a nature to observe, a nature offering continuous discovery, a nature of solitude and wildness, a nature of all scales, a nature both rational and spiritual, a nature that encourages a sense of brotherhood and thus, hopefully, of stewardship.

10

Reflections and Implications

Muir revered the writings of Ralph Waldo Emerson, a fellow Romantic, and, after their brief encounter in Yosemite in 1871, the man himself. Emerson returned the admiration. It is not surprising, then, that some of Emerson's thoughts can be a basis not only for interpreting Muir's outlook on life but also for articulating a Muir-enriched Yosemite experience, a model that might serve for the national parks more generally.

In Emersonian terms, Muir was far from the "mystic" who enfolds minds around the seer's narrow, self-proclaimed vision, but rather more of the "poet" who "unlocks our chains and admits us to a new scene." Emerson speaks with disdain of the common "bards" who savor "wine, mead, narcotics, [and] coffee" to stimulate the intellect to "extraordinary power." Instead he lauds the genuine "poet" whose imagination is the "true nectar" of such intoxication.

Muir spurned even the more modest indulgences of food or drink for sustenance—far from "intoxication"—and committed himself that summer of 1869 to recording faithfully an insight worthy to be seen as the "ulterior intellectual perception" sought by Emerson. Although he did not originally write the journal with the idea of sharing it with others, his highly personal perspective serves well as a guide for our individual engagements with nature, so that we, as he, might stand "one step nearer to things" and "see the flowing or metamorphosis" of nature. In 1836 Emerson apostrophized these lofty words to the poet for whom he "look[ed] in vain":

> Wherever snow falls or water flows or birds fly, wherever day and night meet in twilight, wherever the blue heaven is hung by clouds or sown with stars, wherever are forms with transparent boundaries,

wherever are outlets into celestial space, wherever is danger, and awe, and love,—there is Beauty, plenteous as rain, shed for thee, and though thou shouldst walk the world over, thou shalt not be able to find a condition inopportune or ignoble.

In 1869, Muir seems to have answered the call and translated into a more universal invitation for each of us the dictum of the elder master, becoming himself that very poet.

KNOWER, SAYER, DOER

Yet, Muir is more than poet. Emerson proclaimed three entities in the universe: the Knower (lover of truth), the Sayer (or the Poet, lover of beauty), and the Doer (lover of good). As observer and scientist, Muir was "Knower"; as writer, he was "Sayer"; and as politically active conservationist, he was "Doer," inspiring us all through both his knowledge and words to hear the poetry in nature and respond to its song by taking action to protect it.

During his first Sierran summer, Muir was Knower and Sayer but not Doer, an entity he would become only after "coming down" from the Yosemite Sierra in 1873, and only in response to the urgings of confidants, including Jeanne Carr and Emerson himself. Rather, in his initial years in Yosemite, Muir sought truth and beauty for himself, for his own growth and development, which he later translated into words that help us to see with the clarity of the deep pools of the Merced and with the sharpness of quartz crystals of Cathedral granite, what we, as individuals, might gain from our own "studies" of the Yosemite landscape.

Would Muir see in today's Yosemite visitor the Knower? Clearly, interest in learning about nature exists among the more than four million visitors who enjoy the park each year. Valley Visitor Center and Museum, Happy Isles Nature Center, Ansel Adams studio, Wawona historical complex, Tuolumne Meadows Visitor Center—all crowd with people from opening to closing each day. A rich assortment of books, through the years increasingly variable in sophistication, stand cover to cover across shelves both tall and broad, and presumably are purchased, read, and used in the field. Naturalist walks and campfire programs never lack for eager participants and listeners. Questions of identification—what is that small, darkish bird with a black head that flashes white on its tail as it hops about the campground gleaning crumbs?—commonly follow the Park Service uniform. Even we encounter individuals on the trails

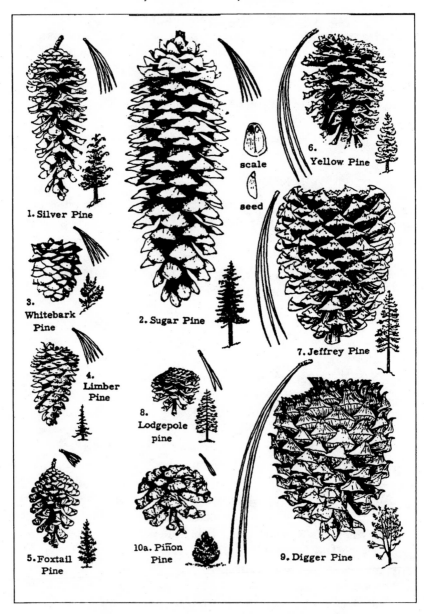

A page from *Sierra Nevada Natural History*. Tracey Storer and Robert Usinger, 1963, *Sierra Nevada Natural History: An Illustrated Handbook.* Berkeley: University of California Press, p. 146. Copyright © 1963 The Regents of the University of California.

who ask us the names of birds or trees. Desire for rational understanding is strong.

And what of the Sayer? Would Muir find the lover of beauty alive and well among Yosemite visitors? Compared to those who pursue the truth of the Knower, still greater numbers of people see Yosemite, particularly the great valley, as a Romantic ideal. This nature for them unrolls as spectacle, as beauty, as an expression of pristine purity. Contrary to Muir's observation that too many fail to raise their eyes to the glories of the valley, today we find more tourists looking up, rather than down, crowding the roads in their vans or RVs, in the shuttle buses or tour trams. The vista points for Bridalveil and Yosemite Falls are typically overwhelmed by people pointing their cameras and camcorders upward toward the vertical walls and wind-blown falls. Only at Glacier Point or Olmsted Point does "downward" describe the common orientation of the gazing visitor. Moreover, many of the trails support a steady stream of walkers—the hot, steep climb to the Vernal Falls bridge and beyond, up the slippery steps of the Mist Trail to the top of Vernal Falls itself, can never be enjoyed in quiet solitude during the summer months, so busy is the path with people of all sizes and shapes, of all ages and physical abilities. Higher still, to Nevada Falls and Half Dome, the linear human flow continues with only slight diminution. In today's world, Muir's "strange experience" might be not in knowing that Professor Butler was in the valley, but in locating him among the crowds on the Vernal and Nevada Falls trails! Nor is the idealization of nature that encourages this sort of visitation restricted to the vastness of the valley's rocks and waters. The frequent appearances of deer and coyotes on the valley floor (bears being less common and less conspicuous than they once were) never fail to command an audience, as do the marmots at Olmsted Point and the California ground squirrels that consistently elicit squealing delight from children of all ages on the sprawling grounds of the Ahwahnee Hotel. All of these expressions of the popularity of Yosemite is testimony to the success of advocates, like Muir himself, who have convinced Americans and foreign visitors alike that the vistas and life of the place are, indeed, the finest manifestations of the natural world, a "novel grandeur," a landscape of "glorious objects" to be admired, even treasured.

In spite of these positive impressions, we think, nonetheless, that Muir still would be disappointed in the modern Yosemite visitors, finding them "caring too little." For many, observation and discovery are secondary to entertainment and comfort. Crowds in the Visitor Centers grow to throngs in the gift shops; quiet contemplation yields to racing bicyclists and noisy rafters or rock climbers; a brief interlude of solitude "gazing into the face of a daisy" succumbs to an afternoon of socializing over an order of pizza. In the Ahwahnee Hotel, bustling with humanity in all seasons, graceful arrangements of huge pink and white lilies, sprays of orchids, and columns of *Liatris* (though not Yosemite natives) would have certainly captured Muir's admiration, but we saw not one person accord the flowers even a glance as the guests strolled from room to restaurant ("coats required for gentlemen"), from lobby to limousine. Vehicle windows frame the typical view of cliff or falls, forest or distant vista; too few visitors perch on rocks or logs in longful wonderment. We see only a handful among the thousands of visitors that we encounter on a given day engaging in more than the most casual nature study, whether observing birds, identifying flowers, studying the sky, or examining rock crystals. Almost no one, moreover, writes or sketches in a notebook, as did Muir for so much of his Yosemite time.

Our own writing has often drawn stares or even inquiry. In fact, the only occasion we recall of seeing what looked like journal writing occurred during a three-hour traffic delay on the Tioga Road well east of Gin Flat caused by a head-on collision (an increasing hazard since Muir's days here) miles beyond, near Crane Flat. With the line of cars and vans sitting stationary, a group of adolescents played games on the pavement; a young family walked a baby on the road shoulder; another set up a barbecue and grilled hot dogs; most travelers reclined their car seats, turned on their radios, and read newspapers. Yet one lone woman left the plush upholstery of her car for an unyielding seat on a nearby boulder and, turning her back from the throng to front the forested valley beyond, took out a pen and opened a notebook, and became quickly absorbed in her thoughts and words. When the traffic eventually resumed, she joined a carload of foreign visitors.

Undoubtedly, Muir would be disheartened by the growth of interest in the individual recreational activities more athletically than spiritually strengthening. He would see rock climbing and hard hiking (Stephen Fox quotes from a journal of Muir: "Hiking is such a vile word. . . . you should saunter through the Sierra"), hang gliding and mountain biking (illegal but nonetheless a practice in Yosemite) as adversarial engagements with nature more than affectionate embraces of "the mountain's heart." Whitewater rafting on the Merced or Tuolumne rivers and windsurfing on Lake Tenaya would impress him as more akin to the thrill-seeking of a county fair amusement ride than to a caring relationship with "divine glories." "As well hammer pitons into the walls of the Sistine Chapel, ride bikes down the aisles of the Notre Dame Cathedral,

Muir sketch of R.U. J. (Ralph Underwood Johnson) and guide examining one of the Tuolumne waterwheels. John Muir papers, Holt-Atherton Department of Special Collections, University of the Pacific Libraries. Copyright © 1984 Muir-Hanna Trust.

or wash in the holy water of the Jordan, as desecrate the sacred temple of Yosemite!" Muir might admonish them.

Even seemingly innocuous activities might seem to Muir to deaden, rather than enhance, the pursuits of the "wanderer [who] enjoys the freedom and glory of God's wilderness." Is it possible that bicycle riding on the floor of Yosemite Valley, formally endorsed by the Park Service and idealized by environmental groups, would impress him as too focused on conveyance, too little on "linger[ing], observing, sketching, taking notes among the glaciated rocks and moraines"? Might sunbathers on beach sand or rafters on a quiet river remind Muir of insensitive and unresponsive sheepherder Billy, especially when the modern recreationists are immersed in the latest Danielle Steele saga, blinded by cosmetic eye shields, or deafened by Walkman plugs. Bicycles, tricycles, Frisbees, footballs, baseballs, paddleballs, hackey sacks—such artifacts of the playground and playing field were not encountered by Muir in his day but undoubtedly would be seen by him as both impediments to the study of nature and sacrilegious to the spiritual experiences offered by the "romantic enchanting beauty and peace" of Yosemite.

Muir expressed no general condemnation of the lodging facilities in the valley—bane to so many modern environmentalists—and even Ralph Waldo Emerson's preference for a hotel room rather than an open camp hardly swayed his admiration for the elder philosopher, "the most serene, majestic, sequoia-like soul I ever met." Yet Muir regretted for himself the need to spend an evening in a "paltry" room of a hotel. For him, the camping spot was critical. It was not simply a place for physical renewal, for subsistence, from which he expected to resume his daytime solitude when the sun rose. Nor was camp a place to return for socialization, as Concord was for Thoreau, who chose to walk back to town almost daily. Neither was it simply a necessity demanded by the "business" of sheep raising. At night, Muir shunned the camp of indifferent Billy and uneasy sheep, preferring instead a more isolated spot from which to admire "the sky like one vast lily meadow in bloom!" For Muir, then, the dark hours extended the time in the "temple."

National park campgrounds (and hotels, for that matter), in Yosemite and elsewhere in the park system, might be so conceived and managed today as to provide better opportunities for continuing the development of the Knower and Sayer in the human mind and heart. They need not be only places of subsistence, socialization, or business. Yet in many cases these functions seem to be paramount. Today's noisy, littered campgrounds, inhabited by people motivated by low fees, concerned with "partying" or "having a good time," are in many respects worse than the sheepherder's camp, and with no excuse. The National Park Service might even be compared with Delaney, hiring a concessionaire and Mystix to tend people like a flock of sheep that bring them their livelihood, penning them up at night and herding them through in the daytime, while concentrating their efforts on preserving the "forage"—

the scenery—to insure the seasonal production of "fleece," the annual influx of visitors. People may not be "hoofed locusts," but certainly they have a tendency to follow the crowd, and perhaps the Park Service— even given the difficult and contradictory political world in which it must function—could be faulted for tending its flock too casually, allowing it to wander too far from the vision of the Sierra's most insightful and sensitive visitor almost a century and a half ago.

Of course, our impressions could underestimate the degree of learning and respectful affection that goes on, but we think not. For Muir, the rational study of the Knower and the marveling wonderment of the Sayer were primary activities—his "recreation"—whether he was carefully noting the structure of a tiny flower or quietly sitting in contemplation, "thinking only of the glorious Yosemite landscape." We see little among modern visitors that suggests such sensitivity to the bountiful treasures to be discovered in nature in Yosemite.

The "truth" of the Knower and the "beauty" of the Sayer—they were one for Muir. The modern mind, however, tends to see them not simply as different, but as polar opposites. Judging by our own decades of experiences with students, we think that a common human reaction is either to admire the apparent precision of science and shun the seeming vagueness of poetry, or to find comfort in the emotive language of the poet and struggle with the objective words of the scientist. Muir muted the distinction, finding beauty in truth and truth in beauty. The challenge to all of us, as Yosemite visitors, is to emulate his fusion of worldviews.

Great gray owl and junco, as sketched by Geraldine Vale

How, though, more specifically, do we meet the challenge? To become a Knower is far easier than in Muir's time. The array of field guides and natural history books, written at all levels of sophistication, allows all of us to pursue truth. If we know little, we can learn much; if we know much, we can learn still more. If we know birds, we can learn insects; if we know rocks, we can learn weather. If we know names, we can ask questions about behaviors, histories, and relationships. If we know one meadow, we can learn another, compare them for similarities and differences, wonder about their pasts and their futures, question their animal inhabitants or their landscape settings. If we recognize sugar pine as a species, we can learn that "every tree calls for special attention." If all looks familiar, we can look again, more intensely, more carefully, more closely—for the fungus beneath the rock, the borer in the bark—to find new knowledge, new truth. None of us need literally "to give [our] li[ves] . . . to read . . . a grand page of mountain manuscript," nor should we need to "bewail our poor inevitable ignorance." It is the progress toward truth, the immersion in the wonder of becoming a Knower, that captures the spirit of Muir.

To become a Sayer is both easier and more difficult than to become a Knower. At its most visceral level, the appreciation of beauty may seem effortless, particularly when confronted with the grandeur of the Yosemite landscape. Yet, like the pursuit of truth, the development of an ability to see beauty requires attention, perhaps even more concentration and self-discipline than that needed for the art of knowing. It is not an idle or casual mind, but a focused and attentive one, that sees and reacts as did Muir: "Bathed in such beauty, watching the expressions ever varying on the faces of the mountains, watching the stars, . . . watching the circling seasons, listening to the songs of the waters and winds and birds, would be endless pleasure."

It is a different world today than in 1869, the rejoinder might be, and no one could be expected to reenact the life of a mid-nineteenth century loner. Muir himself would agree. Cutting fir boughs for beds, picking flowers for lapels, building bonfires for warmth during timber- line nights, camping freely anywhere, taking dogs as companions—such activities are not as acceptable in this more crowded, less wild world. But sleeping on a Therm-a-rest mattress, admiring the flowers where they grow, using propane stoves for cooking, camping in designated sites, leaving pets at home—none of these hinders the search for truth and beauty.

The "recreation" of Muir, his 1869 activities and their contemporary expressions, serve as the means to become, at once, Knower and Sayer.

Reflections and Implications

Preeminent, of course, is observation, looking intensely at the natural world, seeing in that world both truth and beauty. Gentle touch, subtle redolence, "songful" sound, all complement the sense of sight. He sketched, and so might we all; photography seems to be the modern equivalent, but the casual quick snapshot cannot replicate the attentive absorption required of drawing or other more thoughtful image-making. In an especially vivid metaphor, contemporary naturalist Annie Dillard writes of this higher level of "seeing": "When I walk with a camera, I walk from shot to shot, reading the light on a calibrated meter. When I walk without a camera, my own shutter opens, and the moment's light prints on my own silver gut." The writing of a journal, the simple recording of flowers seen or birds observed or weather encountered, the written articulation of engagement with both the Knower's truths and the Poet's beauty—these were the cores of Muir's "recreational activities." To so immerse the senses requires, as it did for Muir, much time and mental effort, conditions necessary to stimulate the human imagination. The "intoxicants" of artificial amusement, thrill-seeking entertainment, or even idle pacification obstruct the melding of Knower and Sayer. Such fusion is what Muir might have hoped "recreation" in Yosemite, and in the wilds of the national parks more generally, would become.

POLICY RECOMMENDATIONS

Individuals, then, may prod themselves to follow in Muir's footsteps and mind set, but centralized commitment might also spur the Yosemite visitor in directions designed to enhance the development of the Knower and Sayer in each of us. As with current Park Service policy, some combination of opportunity, incentive, and coercion might inspire a redefinition of "appropriate" recreation.

Opportunity

The common environmentalist critique of the national parks and their administering agency, the National Park Service, identifies a plethora of faults—the parks focus too much on scenery, too little on biodiversity; the parks remain too small to be "complete ecosystems"; park policy bends toward mass recreation (a criticism that prompts a new name, the National Parking Service); park management stems from false ideals of pristine nature and natural processes, both of which discourage the active manipulation and restoration needed to maintain desirable conditions of biota and landscape. Some truth lies amid these arguments. But

123

hidden within their vituperative and seductive language is a profound fact: America's National Park System represents the most successful, large-scale attempt both to protect nature from the landscape-altering resource development needed to support humanity and to offer people the chance to experience the natural world. No other effort in the history of people compares; no other contemporary attempt is as likely to endure. As a consequence, the opportunity, in Yosemite or in other units of the National Park System, to be one with Muir in spirit, to become Knower and Sayer, is without parallel.

The general accessibility that the parks provide, often a criticism by those committed to untrammeled wilderness, enhances that opportunity. Rather than regretting or even condemning the roads, lodging, and other services found in the parks, we welcome—as did Muir—the possibilities that such facilities make available for visitors both young and old, athletically fit and athletically challenged. Not that we yearn for more development; service facilities in Yosemite appear to us more than adequate. But the contingencies of history and the deliberate planning decisions by the Park Service have created, if not an optimal design of development, one that offers visitors to the Yosemite Sierra rich opportunities to develop individual knowledge and sensitivity. Serious problems lie less with the physically constructed facilities than with how they are used, difficulties that require attention to incentives and coercion.

Incentive

Substantial efforts by the National Park Service presently encourage visitor understanding and appreciation of natural phenomena in Yosemite. These are significantly augmented by the Yosemite Association and Yosemite Institute, private, membership-seeking, nonprofit organizations whose interpretation, education, and management purposes replicate analogue groups in other major units of the National Park System. More incentives could focus attention, however, on the enhancement of knowledge and sensitivity as the primary purpose of Yosemite and other national parks.

Park-specific natural history guides   At one time, the Yosemite visitor could find booklets with a wealth of information about the park's coniferous trees, broadleaf trees, wildflowers, mammals, birds, reptiles and amphibians, geology, and waterfalls. Text and graphics, in photographs and drawings, provided details of how such phenomena might be recognized, why they behaved or appeared as they did, and where they could be found in the Yosemite landscape. The specific references to the Yosemite Sierra enticed visitors to observe, to discover: A sugar pine with a diameter of 8 feet, "one of four large trees of this species on the floor of Yosemite Valley," grows "between the Ahwahnee grounds and the second bridge on the main highway to Mirror Lake"; Pacific dogwood, with "great numbers of large, showy, cream-white blossoms" in spring and "crimson foliage and clusters of shiny red seeds" in fall, attracts people to Yosemite "primarily to enjoy the colorful . . . dogwood displays"; mountain misery is "best seen along the Wawona Road where it forms solid carpets under pines"; long-tailed weasels "have been seen between the Yosemite Museum and the Administration Building a number of times"; western wood pewees, whose "usual forage range is about 15 to 40 feet above the ground," nest in Yosemite forests, arriving "about the second week in May and [departing] about mid-September"; the three species of "blue-bellied lizards" that live in Yosemite each inhabit a different elevation range in the park; Bridalveil Fall decreases in water volume through the summer, and by autumn is "reduced almost to a misty spray, its waters occasionally wafted upward by a sudden updraft from the Valley floor."

Mostly no longer available, these guides apparently have been replaced by regional books on, for example, the mammals of North America, the reptiles and amphibians of the American West, the trees of California, or the natural history of the Sierra Nevada. Greater breadth in topical or regional coverage, although excellent in its own right, necessarily makes more diffficult the identification and understanding of those fewer species and features in Yosemite. Encouraging knowledge and enhancing a sense of place, park-specific booklets, whether provided by the Park Service or the Yosemite Association, belong on the bookshelves of the visitor centers and concession stores.

Broader view of "nature"   Place-specific information is needed for a wider range of natural phenomena. The natural world for which interpretation is provided, whether in Yosemite or other national parks, typically embraces only biological species and geology. Among the myriad living organisms, moreover, attention almost always focuses on vertebrates, while within geology, interpretation usually looks to the long-time scales needed to explain rock origins or to the most obvious glacial or other erosional landforms. "Nature," however, comprises far more—the sky, weather and climate, streamflow, ground water, soil, slope processes, insects or other invertebrates, fungi and other nonvascular plants, rare or extinct plants and animals, interconnections among phenomena, Holocene history, and impacts of modern humans. Some

125

HEATH FAMILY

RED HEATHER
Phyllodoce breweri Heller

Flowers rose-purple, cup-shaped, in terminal clusters. Stems erect, leafy, 6 to 12 inches high. Leaves very narrow, short, thickly crowded around stems. Grows only at higher elevations where they form extensive, showy stands. Also known as Bryanthus.

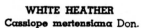

WHITE HEATHER
Cassiope mertensiana Don.

Flowers pure white, bell-shaped, nodding, with tiny red caps. Stems rigid, 1 foot or less high, densely leafy. Leaves very short, closely overlapped in 4 rows. Found along rocky ridges and under ledges near timber-line. Occasionally found as low as Tuolumne Meadows.

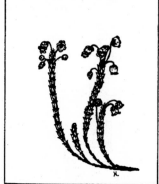

PRIMROSE FAMILY

SIERRA SHOOTING STARS
Dodecatheon jeffreyi Moore

Flowers ¾ to 1 inch long, rose-pink, base yellowish with distinct purple band. Stems naked, 5 to 18 inches high, bearing a cluster of 5 to 15 nodding flowers. Leaves 2 to 15 inches long from base. This and other related species are found commonly throughout the Yosemite region in wet meadows.

Pages from "101 Wildflowers of Yosemite" and "Mammals of Yosemite National Park." M. E. Beatty, C. A. Harwell, and J. E. Cole, 1938, "101 Wildflowers of Yosemite," *Yosemite Nature Notes* (Special Number), 17(6), p. 95. Harry C. Parker, 1952, "Mammals of Yosemite National Park," *Yosemite Nature Notes* (Special Number), 31(6), p. 66.

From "Mammals of Lake Tahoe" by Robert T. Orr. Courtesy of publisher, California Academy of Sciences.

MARMOT

quoia cone is about the size of a hen's egg, the magnitude of this feat is even more impressive.

Since the seeds are what interest the squirrel, obviously the scales and stems of cones make quite a pile of debris after its meals. A spot is usually chosen for the shucking process which provides a good lookout, such as a rock, log or old stump. Consequently the waste from many meals adds up to quite a pile of scales and stems. These piles are known as "kitchen middens" and are readily found throughout the forested country

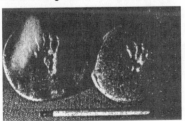

From cast by M. V. Hood

Marmot tracks. Hind foot on left, front on right. Six-inch pencil.

above the rim. Gray squirrels may make similar middens, but with a greater variety of food available, such workings are not found so commonly in Yosemite.

Daytime travelers on the Tioga Road are very likely to make the acquaintance of the **southern Sierra marmot.** Near or within the patches of meadowland, marmots are fond of lying flattened out on the tops of large rocks, basking in the sunshine. About the size of a cat, with its glossy, grizzled, light-brown upperparts and contrasting orange-yellow chest and feet, they make a strikingly pretty sight in this position. Easterners will note a strong resemblance to a woodchuck, for the two are closely related.

It must have plenty of green plants to eat and rocks or trees or logs under which to burrow. Tunneling under such a place means that a predator is not able to dig them out. At the first real threat of danger, it is toward the burrow that the marmot gallops. Some of them take up residence in barren rock slides so that in case of alarm, all they have to do is

expressions of nature, moreover, are better understood and appreciated with visual aids that transcend normal human sight—telescopes enhance the sky; magnifiers, the structure of butterfly wings; microscopes, the hidden life in a drop of pond water. Similarly, the sounds of bird and insect song, of mammal calls, of the unseen night, are all commonly experienced by visitors, yet virtually ignored in interpretive facilities. Most generally, then, the totality of the natural world, both as particular, discrete phenomena and as parts of landscape systems, deserve greater interpretive attention in Yosemite and other national parks.

Greater sophistication in natural history information   The enhanced attention to breadth should be matched by greater depth. People vary in their backgrounds and knowledge; the content of interpretive materials and programs should reflect that variability. In general, the level of sophistication in Yosemite's interpretive opportunities is quite basic, useful mostly for visitors with little familiarity with the natural world. (Exceptions exist: David Gaines's excellent *Birds of the Yosemite Sierra* and N. King Huber's engaging *Geology of Yosemite* both make complex information accessible to the lay, but interested, reader.) More specifically, for example, the professional research pursued in the park should be readily available to visitors. Jan Van Wagtendonk's continuing study of fire in the Yosemite landscape; Albert Parker's survey of forest composition, dynamics, and environmental relationships; Linda Greene's three-volume study of historic resources in the park; published works on black bear dynamics, bird community structure, Yosemite toad declines, ground squirrel dispersal, the diet and habitat of pine marten, Swamp Lake paleoecology, bank erosion along the Merced River in the Valley, topographic influences on vegetation patterns in the Gaylor Lakes basin, Holocene history of high-elevation meadows, late-Pleistocene chronologies of environmental change—all of these appear in the scholarly literature but not in the interpretive message of Yosemite. A closer link between natural history research and interpretive opportunities would serve as an incentive for visitors to become more profound Knowers and Sayers.

Local and continuously updated guides   Just as visitors come to Yosemite with varying backgrounds and thus require greater diversity in interpretive materials, so too are the places within the park variable in both space and time. The environmental conditions at El Portal vary from those in the valley, and these differ from those at Glacier Point, at Tuolumne Meadows, or at Tioga Pass, and the conditions at any one of these single locales varies from week to week, month to month, year to year, decade to decade. Recognition of this variability would enrich the presentation of the park's natural history. Guides to local conditions, updated often to reflect the march of the seasons, would entice visitors to learn about the Yosemite landscape. Short guide leaflets or individual informational sheets could identify natural phenomena at particularly prominent places—at the very least, at Tioga Pass, Tuolumne Meadows, Lake Tenaya, Porcupine Flat, White Wolf, Crane Flat, Hodgdon Meadow, Yosemite Valley, El Portal, Bridalveil Meadows, Glacier Point, Wawona, and each of the High Sierra Camps. The advance of blooming flowers through the summer, the appearance of fungi on the forest floor, the common nesting birds (including such life history events as the hatching of eggs or the fledgling of young), the notable weather and hydrologic events (How wet is it this summer? How much snow fell last winter?)—all such information enriches the Yosemite experience and promotes the development of Knowers and Sayers.

The physical infrastructure needed to gather such timely information would be minimal. Additional daily weather data stations and stream-gauging stations would augment those already in existence. We envision specifically a standard temperature and precipitation recording structure at each of the prominent places in Yosemite. The information so gathered would not only serve the interpretive program but also the research and management needs of the park.

The human commitment would be less than it might seem. Park Service naturalists and rangers, concession personnel, campground hosts, and Yosemite Association volunteers could all contribute. The ability and the willingness to do so should be part of what is expected to be employed or otherwise formally engaged with Yosemite.

Natural history bulletin boards   Expanded and enriched interpretive information calls for increased accessibility; knowledge can act as an incentive to visitors only if it is open and convenient. Natural history bulletin boards—in at least each of the seventeen locales in the park already mentioned—could present the natural history stories that are not offered in other formats, probably occurrences that are immediate, such as unusual sightings of birds, frogs, mammals, or flowers; yesterday's high temperature; or a fire burning on a nearby ridge.

Even more singular natural events that occur in Yosemite could be explained on these bulletin boards. Yosemite Valley's great rock fall in July 1996 serves as an example. We, though in the park when the landslide occurred, learned about it by word of mouth; only a couple of days after the slide did any official recognition of the event appear in public places, such as the Tuolumne Meadows Lodge information board and the White Wolf Campground bulletin board, and even then the message was not one of interpretation but convenience: Visitors were urged to call home and assure loved ones of their well-being, suspiciously an expedience to free busy park phone lines and personnel. Eager to learn about what had happened and what it meant, in terms of the dynamics of the natural landscape of Yosemite, we found ourselves anticipating the morning arrival of the *San Francisco Chronicle*, where, indeed, we found interpretation—the location of the rock fall, the size of the rock mass, the cause of the damage on the valley floor (more from trees blown over by a burst of air pushed outward by the falling rock than by the granite itself), the geomorphic meaning (the rock on the valley walls varies in hardness and thus in propensity to generate rock slides), the frequency of rock falls in Yosemite Valley in the historic past. What an opportunity for the Park Service, rather than for a newspaper from a distant city, to engage visitors, to inform and educate, to generate appreciation for the workings of the natural world!

The information so presented (whether on bulletin boards or in other formats) should, of course, be accurate. One recent summer when we visited Kings Canyon National Park after a winter of one of the heaviest snowfalls on record, the Park Service Visitor Center at Grant Grove had displayed, as the most recent data, the annual snowfall for the previous year, an unusually dry winter season. The personnel with whom we talked made no attempt during our week-long stay to correct the prominent sign, a small matter of changing a few numbers. Our dismay with the Park Service's carelessness was exceeded only by the apparent visitor indifference.

In addition to informing visitors, bulletin boards could also make all of us participants in interpretation. As is common in some local nature centers, opportunities might be provided for visitors to record, and for others to read, what they have seen or otherwise experienced. The visceral interest in such recording cannot be overestimated, judging by the popularity we observed of the general record book at the backcountry camp, Bearpaw, in Sequoia National Park, during our stay there one summer. Taken together, then, the natural history bulletin boards would bring together park naturalists and rangers, administrators and research staff, visitors and employees, all sharing a common commitment to learn about and to generate appreciation for the grand landscape of Yosemite.

Reinstate Yosemite Nature Notes   Increased accessibility of information might include a particular format from the past. For decades. from 1922 to 1961, the Yosemite Natural History Association (which would become the present Yosemite Association) published a subscription and sale-supported periodical, *Yosemite Nature Notes*, in which members of the park community presented short, popular essays on natural history and other topics for the general public. These writings often described the experiences or reported observed phenomena in Yosemite, for instance, geologic history interpreted from the top of Tioga Peak, the location of a particularly large lodgepole pine near Harden Lake, the force of high winds on a particular day on the Sierra crest, glacial moraines and their plants in Dana Meadows, the "wounding" of red fir by mistletoe and bark beetles at Glacier Point, behavioral interactions between a short-tailed weasel and a belding ground squirrel, and a status report on yellow-legged frogs in the park. Modest and simple in format, *Yosemite Nature Notes* provided a means for the Yosemite enthusiast to learn more about the park, to maintain a link to it even at a distance, and to participate in its interpretation. The current quarterly of the Yosemite Association accomplishes some of these purposes, but it is, although an excellent periodical, a bit more formal and does not, in fact, appear on visitor center or store bookshelves.

The resurrection in 1992 of *Nature Notes from Crater Lake,* identical in size and format to the old *Yosemite Nature Notes,* hints of the potential. The several subsequent annual issues enliven Crater Lake National Park with diverse topics—a survey of spotted owls in the park, dynamics of whitebark pine around the crater rim, activity of golden-mantled ground squirrels near the lodge, mammal tracks in the snow, an aquatic study of Whitehorse Ponds, air quality trends in the park, the effects of drought on springs and ponds. The visitor who reads these pages cannot help but feel that Crater Lake is not only "pretty scenery" but also both a landscape abounding with life, rich with natural phenomena worth knowing about, and a place frequented by people who engage and care about it.

Varied venues   Written materials will always remain central to the development of the Knower and Sayer in the Yosemite visitor, but other forms of interpretation would also act as incentives to emulating Muir. First, the existing visitor centers and museums would benefit from attention to presentations that broaden subject matters and deepen content complexity; we would welcome, for example, a return of the fine display of insects that once adorned a wall in the old valley museum.

Second, the present self-guiding nature trails in Yosemite, at least those with which we are familiar, are—the word is not too strong—appalling. The Soda Springs trail at Tuolumne Meadows includes signs worn illegible with age; the conifer trail on the Tioga Road near Porcupine Flat suffers from neglect, the trail lost to wash-outs and the tree species separated from the signs discussing them by the death of old trees and growth of new ones; the Tuolumne Grove trail ignores features along the mile-long descent to the grove itself, prompting at least one visitor we observed to snap a photo of his family gracing a large incense cedar, erroneously assuming it to be a giant sequoia. (Two good examples of the potential for improvement are the trail guide in the valley that interprets "A Changing Yosemite" and the Forest Service nature trail beyond Tioga Pass.) More nature trails—at least a dozen— in more areas with more information—at Tuolumne and Tenaya, in the red fir forest along the Tioga Road, near Bridalveil, and at Chinquapin, trails that pull visitors over a granite ridge, through the forest, beside a meadow, along a valley stretch of the Merced—may be Yosemite's most pressing interpretive need.

Third, library collections accessible to the general public would help visitors pursue natural history questions raised by their field experiences. Such collections could not present all types and levels of information that visitors might desire, but, judging by our own frustration with being denied access to the Yosemite insect collection (an understandable restriction for a research resource) and being offered no other source to help with the identification of a spectacularly structured insect, which we much later confirmed as a long-eared borer, we think that more opportunities could be provided, a provision that in itself could help redefine the Yosemite experience.

Fourth, although contrary to the usual interpretive facilities in national parks, small gardens of labeled plants—at Tuolumne, Crane Flat, Wawona, and El Portal—would resurrect the concept of the wildflower garden behind the museum on the valley floor. Finally, we observe the difficulty of stopping along most stretches of park roads; more paved and maintained pull-outs would entice visitors to observe and discover.

Individual and group experiences   Most of these suggestions for enhanced interpretive opportunities, incentives for visitors to develop themselves as Knowers and Sayers, stress individuals acting on their own: Personal initiative and singular exploration are the essence of Muir's component of discovery. We certainly support enthusiastically, nevertheless, the naturalist-led walks and talks, which serve an essential purpose of encouraging those less knowledgeable, more timid, or otherwise needing or enjoying such group experience. Nonetheless, opportunities for individual activity should be seen as primary, rather than secondary.

Promotion of the Sayer   Enhanced Knowers may tend to become thoughtful Sayers, but more direct encouragements for visitors to develop love of beauty should be conspicuous in the Park Service message.

Not that such incentives are absent now, but contemplative sensitivity is hardly promoted as the ideal Yosemite experience. Perhaps visitors should be reminded at entrance stations of the virtues of quiet, careful observation, and sitting in "dumbfounded admiration." (Currently, a visitor might think that the only important rule in Yosemite is proper food storage, so paranoid is the Park Service about black bears.) Also, a return to an old tradition, the campground ranger, one who lives in a facility at the entrance to each campground, would act to encourage visitor circumspection about what is legal and appropriate in the campgrounds. The volunteer campground host, the present substitute for the campground ranger, we have found mostly inadequate. Unauthorized, unable, or unwilling to enforce even the existing regulations, campground hosts often seem most interested in administering the other rule seemingly pivotal to the Yosemite experience (in addition to proper food storage): the payment of fees. One summer, in fact, a good-natured host in Yosemite actively encouraged the sharing of campground sites, even in excess of the maximum number of vehicles allowed per site, and to this end actually placed strangers together at a single site, without mutual consent! Far from promoting a more sensitive Yosemite experience, then, the campground hosts have at times served an opposing goal. Moreover, on the grounds of Camp Curry and the Yosemite Lodge, where footsteps and bicycles crush plants in most idle land, greater care to landscaping would express, and thus enhance in visitors, greater sympathy toward nature. Overall, the sensitive and gentle encounter with the natural world, the appreciation of beauty, even without the detailed understanding of the Knower, serves the goal of becoming like Muir in the "Yosemite temple."

Coercion

However dedicated to maintaining opportunity and creating incentive, park policy designed to enhance the sensitivity of the Yosemite experience must include coercive regulations. Whereas added restrictions on individual behavior may invite negative reactions—particularly in a time of distrust or even outright hostility to centralized governments acting against laissez-faire individualism—we note that prohibitions commonly characterize American life where the values of seeking knowledge and poetry are central: in classrooms, libraries, museums, and theater halls. Muir himself appreciated the need for governmental coercions against irresponsible individual actions, as suggested by a paraphrase of one of his best-known passages: "Any fool can destroy trees [or the

Mount Dana from the Gaylor Lakes Basin

personality of the Yosemite experience]. . . . God has cared for these trees [and the benevolent landscape of the Yosemite temple]; but he cannot save them from fools,—only Uncle Sam can do that."

Elimination of inappropriate recreational opportunities Environmental groups have long sought to purge the national parks of recreational and other land uses that they have deemed inconsistent with park purposes. Both the principle of restricting what people may do as recreation in national parks and many of the details of those restrictions have become conventional wisdom in today's national park policy. Through the century of Yosemite's existence, restrictive regulations have excluded previously accepted practices and facilities in the name of appropriateness for a national park: growing hay in valley meadows, controlling predators, feeding bears, pasturing nonnative elk, driving vehicles off roads, golfing on a valley course, pushing hot coals from Glacier Point (the "fire fall"), grazing mules and horses on meadows, clearing logs from the Merced River to facilitate rafts and boats. All are now relegated to past park history. Still further exclusions might be considered: the golf course at Wawona, the ski area at Badger Pass, the swimming pools at Camp Curry and the Ahwahnee Hotel, the winter ice-skating rink in the valley. Our criticism of these recreations focuses not on the more usual ecological impacts of these facilities but on their effects on the personalities of both the Yosemite landscape and the Yosemite experience.

Extension of exclusions and restrictions   In order to emphasize further the enhancing of both knowledge and sensitivity as the core of the visitor encounter with Yosemite, park policy should exclude still more recreational facilities and activities. First, bicycles should be banned from the park. Presently, bikes are promoted as an alternative to autos, a promotion based more on the wickedness of the automobile than the virtue of the bicycle. But just as autos were once encouraged as a means of increasing visitation to, and thus political support for, the national parks, the uncritical embrace of the bicycle has sown the seed of an invader with the potential to grow into a problem comparable to the auto. Bicycles are not always ridden as a means to be "close to nature"; rather, many people seem to ride them simply as a vehicle of transportation, much like the automobile, or, even worse, as a means of overcoming the limits of the automobile in heavy traffic, illegally darting around stopped cars, dashing through stop signs, tearing across meadows for shortcuts, riding the trails. Even more in contrast, the auto serves only the purpose of mobility, at least in the parks, but the bicycle appeals to other types of human motivations: speed-seeking, dare-deviling, endurance-testing. Although restricted to the paved roads and bike trails in Yosemite, bicycles turn up almost everywhere. We have encountered them on footpaths in the valley, between the valley floor and the rim, below White Wolf, out from Tuolumne Meadows. We have also observed off-trail use around White Wolf, Yosemite Creek, and Tuolumne Meadows campgrounds. One summer in the eastern end of Yosemite Valley (closed to private automobiles) impromptu bicycle tracks crisscrossed several slopes like those in an off-road vehicle park. In the abstract, bicycles appeal to the senses of peaceful quiet and healthful exercise, of non-polluting locomotion, of small size, but in reality, their actual use too often contradicts the goal of visitors gently encountering nature. Bicycles belong in Breckenridge and Vail, not in the "Yosemite temple."

Second, noise is increasingly a threat to the Yosemite experience. Radios and other music-generating devices should be either prohibited outright or restricted in use so that no one, anywhere, at any time, should be forced to listen to someone else's tunes. We see no reason why the three young men we observed one summer in the Yosemite Village parking lot, vehicle open-doored with engine running, radio blaring rap music, cigarette package wrappers flying from the windows, should be encouraged—dare we say permitted—to be in this, or any, national park. The same holds true for musical instruments, radio-transmitted voices, and loud and boisterous behavior. Precedence exists for restricting what noise people are allowed to make. We noted that after a night-long party in the Tuolumne Meadows campground—one of the most extreme such events that we have ever endured in a national park—two young men were escorted from their site the following morning by a park ranger. Similarly, recreational vehicle generators should not be permitted to be run anytime during the daylight hours, as they are now; if allowed at all, they should be restricted to a couple of midday hours, 1:00–3:00 or 2:00–4:00 P.M. (We both agreed that the campground host who personally dutifully observed the 10:00 P.M. to 8:00 A.M. noise restrictions only to turn on his generator promptly at 8:01 A.M. somehow missed the spirit of the regulation.) Most generally, the campground "quiet hours" of 8:00 or 10:00 P.M. to 8:00 A.M. simply invite noise at other times. Campgrounds should be places where the Knower and Sayer continue their development, thus requiring relative quiet at all times.

Third, still other recreational behaviors and activities, while less intrusive in the lives of nonparticipating visitors, are not Muir-like in their appeal—rafting on the Merced River, windsurfing on Lake Tenaya. These might be prohibited (as hang-gliding has been), not because they are damaging to the environment, not because they are intrinsically undesirable activities, but because they are too seldom means of enhancing knowledge of and sensitivity to the natural world. The well-established endeavors of horse riding and rock climbing similarly seem inappropriate but are so much a part of the traditions of Yosemite recreation that their elimination would be difficult. The recent closure of the stables at White Wolf suggests, however, that further restraints on recreational livestock, perhaps the cessation of short trail rides, might be possible; such restriction, however, should not constrain access, and thus opportunity, by the physically less-able. At the very least, the active encouragement of both recreational livestock and rock climbing should be curtailed. The parallel to sport fishing—no longer promoted by either stocking programs or Park Service literature—hints that the public might accept restraints on even well-established recreational activities.

Fourth, as a general principle, perhaps as human use increases, the range of acceptable activities and opportunities might be curtailed. Yosemite Valley is a candidate for a range of restrictions: a ban on fires in campgrounds and picnic areas, a reduction in the trinkets in gift shops, a cessation of theater presentations. The valley campgrounds and housekeeping cabins (the worst combination of crowding and isolation from nature) might be closed, perhaps replaced by additional tent cabin facilities (which involve less land and concentrate human activity, compared to campgrounds), designed and landscaped to present the natural world of Yosemite at the doorstep and along the access paths. Just as the congestion posed by the private automobile in the valley prompts a discussion of restrictions of its use, crowding should more generally stimulate consideration of other constraints on what is allowed, with guidance from Muir's ideals of knowledge and sensitivity enhancement.

Fifth, and finally, the range of both incentives and coercions must be effectively communicated to the Yosemite public. Too many present regulations are lost in the long newspaper guide to the park and in the short encounter with a ranger at the entrance stations. On paper and in speech, in English and other languages, both the purpose of visiting Yosemite and the rules enhancing that purpose should be clearly presented.

PARK CRITIQUES

Our suggestions for policy relate more obviously to one of the two major critiques of the national parks, the character of human use. Our call for Muir-like nature study and nature appreciation to be the primary human use of national parks echoes the emphasis on recreation that identifies Ronald Foresta's *America's National Parks and Their Keepers* (which urges recognition of the centrality of human use in the management of national parks), Joseph Sax's *Mountains Without Handrails* (which stresses the importance of maintaining park landscapes for the adventuring human spirit), or the Conservation Foundation's *National Parks for a New Generation* (which advocates policies promoting recreational uses not available outside the parks). Perhaps closest to our own view is the classic book of midcentury, Freeman Tilden's *The National Parks: What They Mean to You and Me*, which sees "recreational value" emerging from the pursuit of learning.

Even while relating immediately to thoughts on recreational use of the national parks, our policy proposals also link, by their invocation of the primacy of scientific understanding of natural phenomena, to the second of the usual criteria by which the parks are evaluated, the character of nature protection. The literature in this arena is especially rich. Lary Dilsaver with William Tweed, for example, in their *Challenge of the Big Trees*, an environmental history of Sequoia–Kings Canyon National Parks, applaud the replacement of object protection by scientific, ecosystem management in national park policy. Alfred Runte (in his *National Parks: The American Experience*) decries the lack of greater attention to such management in the history of the national park system but, like

Dilsaver and Tweed, admires (in *Yosemite: The Embattled Wilderness*) the influences of scientists in policy development in Yosemite. Alston Chase (*Playing God in Yellowstone*) and Karl Hess (*Rocky Times in Rocky Mountain National Park*) both criticize the Park Service for its failure to manage actively national park landscapes for biodiversity, instead favoring the maintenance of excessively large numbers of elk.

The two critiques represent the long-recognized, dual purposes of national parks, human use and nature protection. Invariably, these two goals of the parks are cast as opposing and contradictory, although some authors—including Ronald Foresta, mentioned above; Lary Dilsaver in a professional paper on Muir Woods National Monument; and ourselves, in *Time and the Tuolumne Landscape*—recognize the legitimacy of both purposes. The policy suggestions in this book, by urging a closer link between the human recreation and the protected nature, imply a tighter fusion, a more rational compromise, between preservation and use in the parks.

To develop the Knower and the Sayer in each visitor would be a laudable goal for this park and other units in the National Park System. That development—offered, encouraged, and protected by the Park Service—would have the desirable consequence of enhancing, as it did for Muir, the third of Emerson's entities, the Doer. Few visitors could be expected to grow in a Muir-like progression to become national leaders in conservation, but any deeper appreciation of the "good," as Muir found it in the understanding and wonderment of nature, would only secure the future of Yosemite and other national parks as more than trivial playgrounds. Then could we say that we truly emulate Muir, raising our individual spirits and collective voices with him: "I tremble with excitement in the dawn of these glorious mountain sublimities, but I can only gaze and wonder, and, like a child, gather here and there a lily, half hoping I may be able to study and learn in years to come."

Notes

Bibliography

Index

Notes

In the table below, sources for quoted words and phrases are identified by chapter and page of this book and first substantive word or phrase in the quote. Where there are two or more adjacent quotations from the same source, ellipsis points separate the first word of the first quotation and the last word of the final quotation. All quotations not otherwise identified are from Muir, *My First Summer in the Sierra*, Penguin Nature Library edition of 1987. Full citations for other sources are provided in the bibliography.

INTRODUCTION

page	quote	source
3	father	Stanley: 7
	climbing	Ewart: 52
	typical	Orsi: 138
	astounding	Stetson: ix
	radical amateur . . . method	Fox: 81, 187
	radical egalitarianism	Nash: 41
	deep . . . postmodernism	Oelschlaeger: 197, 203
	Mahayana	Turner: xvi
	Divine	Wolfe 1945: ix
4	with each	Ehrlich: ix
	stern	Ehrlich: ix
	light	Ehrlich: xi
	glorious . . . cell of us	Muir in Ehrlich: xii
	took on grace	Ehrlich: x
	clean . . . etched	Ehrlich: xi
	absorb	Ehrlich: xi
	ramble	Ehrlich: xii–xiii
	important . . . surrender	Ehrlich: xi
5	Godliness . . . ousels	Ehrlich: xiii

CHAPTER 3: OBSERVATION

fine   60

CHAPTER 4: DISCOVERY

page	quote	source
41	A Grand	102
	to the high	86
	romantic	68
	part and parcel	83
	to know . . . better	89
	flattened . . . pastures	86, 87
42	Eating . . . delightful	106
	fine spicy . . . creek	106
	spend[ing]	89–90
	in size	88
	Here	88
	the largest . . . better	88–89
	Three pines	93
	a grand	94
	man alone . . . one	95
	seem to care	104
	dullest eye . . . paradise	98
	come higher	86
	What landscapes	100
44	A fine	101
	And with what	101
	discovery . . . landscape	103
	a grand . . . try	102
	sauntering	103
	external . . . tingling	102
	continuous	106
	dizzy precipices	106
	a yet finer	107
	What rich	110
46	tree lover's	98
49	a small brook	87
	the finest	103
50	how old	89
	to know	89
52	superb . . . ground	98
	charming	93
	[It is] another fine	99
	dipping . . . speed	99, 100
53	rejoicing	102

CHAPTER 5: WILDNESS

	blessed	195
64	thinking	122
	studying	178
	sketching	122
	oftentimes	132
	devoutly . . . tenderness	133
69	radiant resiny	52
	oftentimes	132
	swinging	138

CHAPTER 6: SOLITUDE

page	*quote*	*source*
70	Out of Sight	103
	nip[ping]	98
	What fine	104
	timid	111
	a piece	77
	in parties	98
71	seem to care	104
	A strange	98–99
	over the greater	105
	may become	103
	sauntering	103
	made haste . . . enjoyed	115
	out of sight	103
72	glorious	104
	human mark	103
74	endless	Muir, *Our National Parks*: 97
	out of sight	103
	spicy	106
	an altar . . . gift	48–49
75	What	147
	apparently	146
	precious	48–49
	hard to place	129
	hospitable	241

CHAPTER 7: ALL THINGS, ALL SCALES

page	*quote*	*source*
76	Gazing into	153
	up and away	155
	the sculpture	14

85	devil's slides	150
	axis of the range	149
90	vast show	149

CHAPTER 8: RATIONAL ROMANTICISM

page	*quote*	*source*
91	The Natural	191
	strange	178
	supernatural	180
92	one well-defined	180
	spirit-rappings	180
	trying to draw	178
	had not the	180
93	drawn	178
	strange	179
	common	178–79
	desperately	181
	never	179
	transcendental	180
	clean pairs	181
	gloomy . . . garb	181
	quoting . . . gloaming	185
	strange	186
	compelled	186–87
	everyday	180
	making hay	181
	so little	190
	were looking down	190
	that he must	190
94	Yet respectable-looking	190
	it seems supernatural	190
	regular . . . trees	187
	these noble	193
	Hawthorne	191
97	The natural	191
98	the wreck	Whitney in Colby: xvii
99	winter daisies	Muir, *Mountains of California*: 106
	the noble	116
	harmonious	180
	the natural	191
	marvelous	191

CHAPTER 9: BROTHERHOOD

page	*quote*	*source*
100	More and More	243
	typical	229
	perfect	204
	flowery	234
	When we try	157
	One fancies	157
101	wisely, sternly	142
	Fear not!	174
	endowed . . . sympathy	155
	like to live	204
	should like	212
	the most	198
	Of all	234
102	Probably more	235
	weather so fine	234
	Range of Light	236
	a new heaven	213
	by parting	235
	observing	220
	to study mountain	196
	to study the fine	247
	study glacial	248
	universe	204
	How delightful	252
	not a trace	238
	The whole	238
	money . . . gardens	195
	Were bears	211
	make any	258–59
103	walking	195
	wildest	214
	not a whit	226
	How glad I was	219
	It's coming	220
	Perhaps if	226
	How glad I should be	217
	not a single	217
	recall[s]	221
	filled with	221
	indeed	222
	Who could	224

	tremendous	222
	in all sorts	224
	apparently coming	223
	rising abruptly	228
	greatly enjoyed	229
	Glad to get	229
	How interesting	240
	How delightful	252
104	And lo, here	250
	listening, admiring	250
	this big, divine	252
105	merrily down	230
106	three-feet . . . sod	230
	I emerged	203
107	sings merrily	230
	huge day[s]	102, 103
108	the north rim	243
	the peaks	247
109	A new	213
	the highest	252
110	should like	212
111	the finest	153
112	How interesting	240–41
	perhaps if	226
113	the most	198
	To let sheep	204

CHAPTER 10: REFLECTIONS AND IMPLICATIONS

page	*quote*	*source*
114	unlocks	Emerson: 219–20
	bards . . . power	Emerson: 216
	poet . . . nectar	Emerson: 216
	ulterior	Emerson: 212
	one step	Emerson: 212
	look[ed]	Emerson: 221
	Wherever	Emerson: 224
115	Knower	Emerson: 205
118	Hiking	Muir in Fox: 120
119	wanderer	186–87
120	linger[ing]	220
	romantic	68
	the most serene	Wolfe 1938: 436
	the sky	96

121	thinking	178
122	every tree	51
	to give	102
	bewail	102
	Bathed	213
123	When I walk	Dillard: 31
125	one of four . . . Lake	Cole: 31
	great numbers . . . displays	Brockman 1947: 25
	best seen	Beatty, Harwelt and Cole: 89
	have been seen	Parker: 89
	usual forage . . . September	Beatty and Harwell: 18
	blue-bellied	Walker: 19
	reduced	Brockman 1945: 19
133	Any fool	Muir, *Our National Parks*: 365
138	I tremble	110–11

Bibliography

Beatty, M. E., and C. A. Harwell. 1938. Birds of Yosemite. *Yosemite Nature Notes* (Special Number) 17 (1).

Beatty, M. E., C. A. Harwell, and J. E. Cole. 1938. 101 Wildflowers of Yosemite. *Yosemite Nature Notes* (Special Number) 17 (6).

Brockman, C. F. 1945. Principal Waterfalls of the World and Their Relation to Those in Yosemite National Park. *Yosemite Nature Notes* (Special Number) 24 (1).

Brockman, C. F. 1947. Broadleaved Trees of Yosemite National Park. *Yosemite Nature Notes* (Special Number) 26 (1).

A Changing Yosemite. [1979] 1993. Yosemite National Park: Yosemite Association.

Chase, Alston. 1987. *Playing God in Yellowstone: The Destruction of America's First National Park*. San Diego: Harcourt, Brace, Jovanovich.

Colby, William E, ed. 1960. *John Muir's Studies in the Sierra*. San Francisco: Sierra Club.

Cole, James E. 1939. Cone-bearing Trees of Yosemite National Park. *Yosemite Nature Notes* (Special Number) 18 (5).

Conservation Foundation. 1985. *National Parks for a New Generation*. Washington, D.C.: Conservation Foundation.

Dillard, Annie. 1974. *Pilgrim at Tinker Creek*. New York: Harper's Magazine Press.

Dilsaver, Lary. 1994. Preservation Choices at Muir Woods. *Geographical Review* 84:290–305.

Dilsaver, Lary, and William Tweed. 1990. *Challenge of the Big Trees: A Resource History of Sequoia and Kings Canyon National Parks*. Three Rivers, Calif.: Sequoia Natural History Association.

Ehrlich, Gretel. 1987. Introduction to *My First Summer in the Sierra*, by John Muir. New York: Penguin Books.

Emerson, Ralph Waldo. 1990. *Selected Essays, Lectures, and Poems*. New York: Bantam.

Ewart, Arthur. 1986. Spiritual Sauntering. *Sierra* 71 (4):48–52.

Bibliography

Foresta, Ronald. 1984. *America's National Parks and Their Keepers*. Washington, D.C.: Resources for the Future.

Fox, Stephen. 1985. *The American Conservation Movement: John Muir and His Legacy*. Madison: University of Wisconsin Press.

Gaines, David. 1992. *Birds of Yosemite and the East Slope*. Mammoth Lakes, Calif.: Artemisia Press.

Hess, Karl. 1993. *Rocky Times in Rocky Mountain National Park: An Unnatural History*. Niwot, Colo.: University Press of Colorado.

Huber, N. King. 1987. The Geologic Story of Yosemite National Park. *United States Geological Survey Bulletin 1595*. Washington, D.C.: Government Printing Office.

Muir, John. [1894] 1961. *The Mountains of California*. Reprint, New York: Doubleday Anchor.

Muir, John. 1901. *Our National Parks*. Boston: Houghton Mifflin.

Muir, John. [1911] 1987. *My First Summer in the Sierra*. Reprint, New York: Penguin.

Nash, Roderick Frazier. 1989. *The Rights of Nature: A History of Environmental Ethics*. Madison: University of Wisconsin Press.

Nature Notes from Crater Lake. Crater Lake, Ore.: Crater Lake Natural History Association.

Oelschlaeger, Max. 1991. *The Idea of Wilderness: Prehistory to the Age of Ecology*. New Haven: Yale University Press.

Orsi, Richard. 1985. "Wilderness Saint" and "Robber Baron": The Anomalous Partnership of John Muir and the Southern Pacific Company for the Preservation of Yosemite National Park. *Pacific Historian* 29 (2–3):136–56.

Parker, Harry C. 1952. Mammals of Yosemite National Park. *Yosemite Nature Notes* (Special Number) 31 (6).

Runte, Alfred. 1979. *National Parks: The American Experience*. Lincoln: University of Nebraska Press.

Runte, Alfred. 1990. *Yosemite: The Embattled Wilderness*. Lincoln: University of Nebraska Press.

Sax, Joseph. 1980. *Mountains without Handrails: Reflections on the National Parks*. Ann Arbor: University of Michigan Press.

Stanley, Millie. 1985. John Muir in Wisconsin. *Pacific Historian* 29 (2–3):7–15.

Stetson, Lee, ed. 1994. *The Wild Muir: 22 of John Muir's Greatest Adventures*. Yosemite National Park: Yosemite Association.

Storer, Tracy, and Robert Usinger. 1963. *Sierra Nevada Natural History: An Illustrated Handbook*. Berkeley: University of California Press.

Tilden, Freeman. 1955. *The National Parks and What They Mean to You and Me*. New York: Alfred A. Knopf.

Turner, Frederick. 1988. Foreword to *My First Summer in the Sierra*, by John Muir. San Francisco: Sierra Club.

Bibliography

Vale, Thomas, and Geraldine Vale. 1994. *Time and the Tuolumne Landscape: Continuity and Change in the Yosemite High Country*. Salt Lake City: University of Utah Press.

Walker, M. V. 1946. Reptiles and Amphibians of Yosemite National Park. *Yosemite Nature Notes* (Special Number) 24 (1).

Wolfe, Linnie Marsh, ed. 1938. *John of the Mountains: The Unpublished Journals of John Muir*. Madison: University of Wisconsin Press.

Wolfe, Linnie Marsh. 1945. *Son of the Wilderness: The Life of John Muir*. New York: Alfred Knopf. Reprint, 1987, Madison: University of Wisconsin Press.

Yosemite Nature Notes. Yosemite National Park: Yosemite Natural History Association.

Index

157

Index

160

rules in, 137; success of, 123–24. *See also* Yosemite

National Park Service: compared with Delaney, 120–21; interpretation program of, 124

Nature: change in, 99; guides, 124–25, 128–29; interpretation of, 124, 131–32; meaning of, 125–28; protection of, 137–38; sophisticated knowledge of, 128; trails, 131–32. *See also* Landscape

Nature Notes from Crater Lake, 131

Nevada Falls, 94, 117

Night: experiences in, 75; for Muir, 74

Noise, 135–136. *See also* Campgrounds

North Dome: photo of, 65; trail to, 63–68; mentioned 12, 58, 92

North Fork of Merced River: described, 35–40; photo of, 37

Notebook, 22, 89, 110, 111, 118

Notre Dame Cathedral, 118

Nutcracker, Clark's 19, 80, 82

Nuthatch, red-breasted, 53

Nuthatch, white-breasted, 40

Oak: black, 17, 25, 39, 47, 97 (photo of), 98 (photo of); blue, 17, 25, 30, 31, 35; canyon live, 94; huckleberry, 60, 64, 65, 72, 90; interior live, 32, 35, 36; mountain live, 25–26; valley, 32

Oakdale, 34

Olmsted Point, 19, 117

Onion, 74, 105

Opportunity in park policy, 123–24

Orchard at Bower Cave, 35, 36

Orchid, 47, 118

Owl, great gray: at Crane Flat, 47–48; sketch of, 121; mentioned, 19

Owl's clover, 39

Oxytheca, 44

Park. *See* National parks; Yosemite

Parker, Albert, 128

Past: obscuring causes, 97–98

Pedicularis, 106

Penstemon, 39, 65, 74, 88, 106

Pewee, western wood, 35, 105, 125

Phacelia, 35, 53

Phlox, 46

Pilot Peak Ridge, 21, 41, 45

Pine: digger, 25, 31–32, 33 (photo of), 35; Jeffrey, 17, 51 (photo of), 60, 64, 65, 66, 72; lodgepole, 17, 44, 53, 59, 63, 80, 96 (photo of), 105, 106, 131; ponderosa, 17, 33, 35, 38 (photo of), 98 (photo of); sugar, 17, 25, 35, 47, 49, 51 (photo of), 125; western white, 72, 77; whitebark, 17, 77

Pine cones, 116

Pine drops, 39

Pine marten, 128

Pino Blanco: sketch of, 23; mentioned, 32

Pipet, water, 109

Plane jet trails, 35

Pleistocene, 12, 128

Poison oak, 27, 32, 35, 36, 39

Policy recommendations, 123–38

Poppy, California, 35

Porcupine Creek, 80

Porcupine Creek campground, 63

Porcupine Flat, 17, 59, 63, 129, 131

Prynne, Hester, 91

Quail: California, 32; mountain, 72

Queen Anne's lace, 46

Rabbit, 31

Rafting, 118, 120, 134, 136

Rain: at Hazel Green Creek, 48–49; at Indian Canyon Creek, 62; Muir's description of, 56–57, 62; at red fir camp, 56–57; in summer, 34; mentioned, 88, 107

Raindrops (photo of), 63, 73

"Range of Light," 102

Rappaccini, Beatrice, 91

Index

Yosemite, 111; Yosemite Creek, 53, 54 (photo of)

Sulphur, yellow (butterfly), 109

Summer heat, 29–30

Sunbathing, 120

Supernatural, 91–94

Swallow, 35

Swallowtail: tiger, 32; yellow, 35, 40

Swamp Lake, 128

Swift, white-throated, 74

Swimming pools, 134

Tamarack Flat: Muir's description of, 52; mentioned, 41, 73. *See also* Streams: Tamarack Creek

Tanager, western, 45

Tenaya Canyon, 64

Tenaya Lake, sketch of walk along, 89; Vales at, 88–90; mentioned, 55, 80, 88, 100, 129, 132

Tenaya Peak, 88

Theater, 136

Thistle, 35, 47

Thoreau, Henry David: and battle of the ants, 24; and human socializing, 120

Thunderstorm. *See* Rain

Tilden, Freeman, 137

Tioga Pass, 15, 17, 34, 101 (photo of), 108, 128, 129

Tioga Peak, 131

Tioga Road: abandoned, 63, 67; solitude along, 72–74; traffic stopped on, 118; mentioned, 49, 59, 63, 72, 80

Titmouse, plain, 32

Toad, Yosemite, 128

Tourists: on climbing, 86; indifferent to nature, 53, 83, 85, 113; as Knowers, 115–17, 122; looking downward, 117; Muir's attitude toward, 42, 55, 70–71, 93; at Olmsted Point, 82; as Sayers, 117–21, 122; and warblers, 83

Towhee, 32, 40

Toyon, 32

Trees: falling, 106; learned by child, 95; Muir's appreciation for, 25–26. *See also* names of specific species

Tuolumne Grove, 132. *See also* Sequoia, giant

Tuolumne Meadows: photo of, 104, 112; mentioned, 15, 17, 20, 100, 128, 129, 131, 132

Tuolumne River, 15, 21, 29, 104, 108

Turkey mullein, 30, 31, 35

Turner, Frederick, 113

Tweed, William, 137

Vail (Colorado), 135

Vale, Geraldine (photo of), 8

Vale, Thomas (photo of), 7

Vegetation: altered since 1869, 17–18; in Sierra, 15–18. *See also* Forest; Landscape; Meadows; names of specific plant species

Vernal Falls, 93, 94, 117

Violet, 27, 59

Vireo, 19, 40

Visitor Centers, 115, 117, 131

Vulture, turkey, 31

Wagtendonk, Jan von, 128

Wallflower, 88

Warbler: hermit, 53; McGillivray's, 49; Wilson's, 83, 88; yellow, 40; mentioned, 19

Water ouzel. *See* Dipper

Water strider, 45

Waterwheels of Tuolumne River (sketch of), 119

Wawona, 115, 129, 132

Wawona Road, 125

Weasel: long-tailed, 125; short-tailed, 131

Weather: data, 130; Muir description of, 22–24; recording stations, 129. *See also* Climate; Clouds; Rain